" ● "

i

Toi Derricotte

new and selected poems

To

new and se

Pitt Poetry Series   *Ed Ochester, Editor*

Derricotte

ected poems

University of Pittsburgh Press

Published by the University of Pittsburgh Press, Pittsburgh, Pa., 15260

Copyright © 2019, Toi Derricotte

Manufactured in the United States of America

Printed on acid-free paper

10 9 8 7 6 5 4 3 2

ISBN 10: 0-8229-4566-5
ISBN 13: 978-0-8229-4566-6

Cover Photo: Ted Rosenberg
Cover Design: Joel W. Coggins

For the beautiful children—
Tony, Elliot, Cami, and Julean

and for Cave Canem

and for the mothers and fathers—
Galway, Lucille, Ruth, and Audre

and for Pearl London
and Naomi Long Madgett

CONTENTS

• • • The Empress of the Death House • • •

• • • **Natural Birth** • • •

• • • **Captivity** • • •

• • • Tender • • •

• • • The Undertaker's Daughter • • •

Preface to the New and Selected Poems

•　　•　　•

> The purpose of poetry is to remind us
> how difficult it is to remain just one person.
>
> CZESLAW MILOSZ

Speculations about "I"

I.

I didn't choose the word—
It came pouring out of my throat
Like the water inside a drowned man.
I didn't even push on my stomach.
I just lay there, dead (like he told me)

& "I" came out.
(I'm sorry, Father.
"I" wasn't my fault.)

II.

(How did "I" feel?)

Felt almost alive
When I'd get in, like the Trojan horse.

I'd sit on the bench
(I didn't look out of the eyeholes
So I wouldn't see the carnage).

III.

(Is "I" speaking another language?)

I said, "I" is dangerous.
But at the time I couldn't tell
Which one of us was speaking.

IV.

(Why "I"?)

"I" was the closest I could get to the
One I loved (who I believe was
Smothered in her playpen).

Perhaps she gave birth
To "I" before she died.

V.

I deny "I,"
& the closer
I get, the more
"I" keeps receding.

VI.

I found "I"
In the bulrushes
Raised by a dirtiness
Beyond imagination.

I loved "I" like a stinky bed,

While I hid in a sentence
With a bunch of other words.

VII.

(What is "I"?)

A transmission through space?
A dismemberment of the spirit?

More like opening the chest &
Throwing the heart out with the gizzards.

VIII.

(Translation)

Years later "I" came back
Wanting to be known.

Like the unspeakable
Name of God, I tried

My 2 letters, leaving
The "O" for breath,

Like in the Bible,
Missing.

IX.

I am not the "I"
In my poems. "I"
Is the net I try to pull me in with.

X.

I try to talk
With "I," but "I" doesn't trust
Me. "I" says I am
Slippery by nature.

XI.

I made "I" do
What I wasn't supposed to do,
What I didn't want to do—
Defend me,
Stand as an example,
Stand in for what I was hiding.

I treated "I" as if
"I" wasn't human.

XII.

They say that what I write
Belongs to me, that it is my true
Experience. They think it validates
My endurance.
But why pretend?
"I" is a kind of a terminal survival.

XIII.

I didn't promise
"I" anything & in that way
"I" is the one I was most
True to.

“ ● ”

i

Toi Derricotte   *new and selected poems*

joy is an act

of resistance

<small>From "The Telly Cycle"</small>

After all those years of fear and raging in my poems

How I thrived from the trifles
in my aunt Lenora's handbag—Tums,
pencils, Lifesavers, fancy
colored cards—how, in the early morning
before dawn, before
my parents rose, her welcoming sheets
hid me from the house's
storms. She'd listen to
my far-fetched tales
while I (standing on a stool) "helped"
her dry dishes; or, after, when we'd
walk through the neighborhood's
deep night, with her
teaching me the stars. Or,
from the time I was three
in the printing department
where she worked—my first job
was to watch eagle-eyed and snatch
errant pages from the thundering
printing press (for 10 cents an hour);
our lunches (as exciting as a rendezvous)
at the Broadway Market—corned beef
with fruit punch and a new dill.
The innumerable dresses and coats
she paid months for, in boxes
with large blue ribbons
and tissue paper, believing
in my astounded body's signs—
that I could be a beautiful woman.

All the years
of fear and raging
in my poems, the years I continued
in thankless silence—until I was empty
of it . . .

A slice of almond cake
from the childless woman next door, a few
fried chicken wings from the mother of a
girl whose name I don't remember, who fried
chicken the way they must fry it in heaven.

It took so many years, the self
breaking like a pod, so many years
to pull up the details
of cruelties that were so quickly
buried—so that one could go on!—to bring all that
to consciousness, to hold that pain
until it writes a poem, to hold it
for years until you learn both
the holding and the writing, to
hold it like my father made me
hold still my knee when he put the iodine
on it, to hold it
in consciousness while emotions fill up
to the brain's pinnacle, then, to learn
to feel again in thin streaks—like the dissolving streaks
of a meteor—to see in brief
flashings a form, prying
at memory, fitting each recognition
to a hundred words. You,
the seamstress; you, the parent-
killer; you, the lover,

until all that was never said is
said and said so perfectly
that time itself
changes, as if you
emptied the universe,
and everything started—
but again.

After the Gwendolyn Brooks reading

She sits at the book-signing table with a colorful
African wrap tied around her head, her chin
in her palm, elbow on the table, as if resting her brain
(that silvery Jell-O in its luminous oyster shell), listening
intently to each one of the women who have
come on a church bus in large church hats. They squeal
with joy as they hand her bedraggled books
taken down from their most honored shelves;
and she, who conceived of Maud Martha (that woman who, by sparing
a kitchen mouse, discovered, unfurling, her own great wings
of compassion), talks to each one, letting them
take as many pictures as they like, sandwiched between them—
small, dignified, and perfectly at ease.

Among school children

A great poem is an
unlocked door. Forty years ago,
in Newark, I recited a poem
by heart to fourth graders—
Stanley Kunitz's "The Portrait."

It begins, *My mother never forgave my father*
for killing himself, and goes on
to unbury that sorrow
from deep in his body:

When I came down from the attic
with the pastel portrait in my hand
of a long-lipped stranger
with a brave mustache
and deep brown level eyes,
[my mother] ripped it into shreds
without a single word
and slapped me hard (rhyming
the d's in "word"
and "hard" which, like a slap,
cracks the heart), and ending,

In my sixty-fourth year
I can feel my cheek
still burning.

That year, as in many others,
four children had died
in apartment fires (faulty wiring,
kerosene heaters, no smoke alarms,

doors and windows barred
to keep robbers out
had locked the burning in).

Jermaine Grier told us
his mother had been found
dead in an empty lot. He listened
to the Kunitz poem
and when I said take up
your pencil, he wrote:

Pain is to feel with fear.
Sight is to see things you never saw before.
To hear is to hear sound to develop feeling.
To feel is to touch with feeling.

There was drop-dead silence.

Where is he today? Jermaine
Grier, a boy who once heard
a poem and followed it
out of the burning place within.

As my writing changes I think with sorrow of those who couldn't change

I am thinking with sorrow of those who couldn't change,
of those who committed suicide, of Plath, Sexton, Berryman,
Hemingway with the gun in his mouth;
Ralph Ellison, who would not support young black writers—
they weren't good enough, he said, not as good as he was—
but never finished his second book;
Anatole Broyard, who couldn't write the autobiographical novel
he had been paid to write
because he couldn't write the first truth—
that all those years he had been drama critic
for the *New York Times*, he had been passing for white.
And there are those who face the truth the first time,
but, when that truth changes, can't do it again,
as if the old truth has made
a self so vain they can't let it go.
And I think of the great writers who DO change:
Jerry Stern, in his 90s, writing two new books a year—
his publishers can't keep up!—
poetry; and prose that I love as much as the old awarded
poetry books, because it bares
the movement of a brilliant mind.

Biographia Literaria Africana

I don't know why poets love me! Famous
poets, great writers who treat me

as if I'm their equal. In my childhood,
they called me D-head; they said my feet

were gunboats. "Sing so-
lo," they said, "so low

we can't hear you." But

in the pictures I can see that
little light of glad living in my eyes.

Blessed angels

How much like
angels are these tall
gladiolas in a vase on my coffee
table, as if in a bunch
whispering. How slender
and artless, how scandalously
alive, each with its own
humors and pulse. Each weight-
bearing stem is the stem
of a thought through which
aspires the blood-metal of stars. Each heart
is a gift for the king. When
I was a child, my mother and aunts
would sit in the kitchen
gossiping. One would tip
her head toward me, "Little Ears,"
she'd warn, and the whole room
went silent. Now, before sunrise,
what secrets I am told!—being
quieter than blossoms and near invisible.

Elegy for my husband

Bruce Derricotte, June 22, 1928–June 21, 2011

What was there is no longer there:
Not the blood running its wires of flame through the whole length
Not the memories, the texts written in the language of the flat hills
No, not the memories, the porch swing and the father crying
The genteel and elegant aunt bleeding out on the highway
(Too black for the white ambulance to pick up)
Who had sent back lacquered plates from China
Who had given away her best ivory comb that one time she was angry
Not the muscles, the ones the white girls longed to touch
But must not (for your mother warned
You would be lynched in that all-white town where you grew up—
The one, the only good black boy)
All that is gone—
The muscles running, the baseball flying into your mitt
The hand that laid itself over my heart and saved me
The eyes that held the long gold tunnel I believed in
The restrained hand in love and in anger
The holding back
The taut holding

The enthusiast

Tweezers & a magnifying mirror
Exaggerate the pores   a black hole opens

& pulls my face in   a force so great that
My face   is pulled apart   crushed

Like vanilla wafers (which my mother shaped into pie crusts!)
All those little fragments but one with a hair   thick & black   like a

Primeval forest   that I whack at   though it runs away   I

Go at it   like sex   with all my senses   including my hatred
Of the beast in me   (though it is sometimes as small

As a zygote). Have you ever scrubbed your chin & felt

(With the fat part of your palm) a relentless

Insurgent?

I learned this   from my mother

With what enthusiasm   she took up her weapons

The exchange

The iridescent skin of a swimmer
Pulled out further by the moon

Gifts from the dead

A student said, I've been studying
your line breaks and can't figure out
how they work. I couldn't
explain. All those years they
fought their way to the surface
like cats in a bag. But Lucille
must have given me
breath, because after she died, I
noticed my lines
started to look
a lot like hers! She had told me,
when you lose the flesh
you gain more power. In fact,
that's the only gold
a poet counts on: the power
to give it away. When Ruth Stone
died, she gave me
a new way
to pick up words, like those
silver claws in grocery
stores that pick up
stuffed animals and this time they
don't leap away. Ruth had said, just
put your hand
up in the universe and a poem
will jump in. It's crazy
to trust yourself
like that! But, now,
I'm learning how
to live.
Even when she was getting chemo

twice a week, Lucille would go
anywhere they asked—Australia, Alaska—
carrying her thirty-pound purse, which she would never
give up. No matter how we
warned her, she
did it for nothing! On her deathbed, she wouldn't leave
until her daughters promised,
We'll be all right. You can let go.
       Ruthie, starlit, ribboned
and silked, fragile-skinned, like a coat from a Chinese
wardrobe in the Middlebury
Goodwill, told us
she wasn't going to
die. That evening,
after we sank her
down in the hole they had
clawed out that morning,
we sat around the table
where Marcia had planed
the pine slats of her casket
just the day before (her last words,
Marcia said, spoken really
to herself, *Everyone
has to die*), spooning her favorite—
Kozy Shack rice pudding—
right out of the plastic.

Glimpse

Black woman as Magician at CVS

The old woman at the counter sticks her hand in the well of her purse
and sorts through the lumpy dark, pulling out everything she owns
(except money)—a photo of a grandchild, an empty pill bottle, an
outdated coupon—each with a story that she reports to the uninspired
clerk. Finally she pays, turns with her bagged prescription and notices
the long-faced girl behind her, neatly braided and still so small she
fits the tent between her father's thighs. "Got a piggy bank?" she asks,
whisking out a stack of singles. She lands one—like a card shark—
flat in the girl's upturned palm.

• • •

The most surprising and necessary ingredient
in my mother's spaghetti sauce

Two cans of those soggy-looking mushrooms that,
for some reason, after hours of simmering, stay

whole, like belly buttons, and give up a woody essence
that fresh mushrooms do not.

• • •

Bad Dad

I thought I had murdered
my brutish father, but here he is
on TV, risen,
with orange Technicolor hair.

• • •

Glimpse

Before he closed the deal, he decided to check it out—"Well, since I'll be here
a long time, let me see if I like it"—and he plopped down on the earth, feet
crossed, arms propped under his head. I tried it myself, lying face up on
top of him. It *was* a perfect corner of the sky, bluer than cornflowers, with
fast-moving puffs of whiteness skimming the tops of two splendid pines.

I count on you invisible

I count on you invisible
presence   sherbet-colored &
tender receiver, ear
of tissuey blossoms. Who
speaks to me before sunrise? Who
comes with the thunder
of queens? Transparent
gesture   for me
who is made of words.

I give in to an old desire

I lost so much
of the world's beauty, as if I were watching

every shining gift
on its branch with one eye. Because

I was hungry. Because I was waiting

to eat, a self

crawling about the
world in search

of small things. I remember a small thing, my mother's hat,

a tea
hat or cocktail

hat that sat on top of her
perfect face—petals, perhaps

peonies, flaming out, like
the pink feathers of some exotic

bird. Her mother
had been a cook in the South. She grew up

in the home of
wealthy white people. Hesitant

toward her own
beauty, unable

to protect mine, there were things
she never talked about. She said silence

was a balm. It sat
on top of her head, something of exaltation

and wonder exploding
from the inside like

a woman in orgasm. One artificial flower

I have desired
to write about for years.

The intimates

The intimates

In the stalls, we ladies hear
each other pee. I watch her
feet. Unashamedly, she
unrolls the toilet paper, *thrump, thrump, thrump.*
Her shoes are
sturdy beige—*perhaps she's a librarian?*
She definitely has a job!—and she pees
solidly, in a forceful stream
that ends with a quick,
assured finish.

• • •

On a woman who excuses herself from the table, even in restaurants, to brush her teeth

I would feel strange to brush my teeth in public, like I was fouling the
sink more than with an ordinary washing. It's true, you might get shit
on your hands. Still the hands are such pretty little things to wash, so
visible and pink or brown, not at all like the hidden places that you
must scour, digging out threads of meat and torn, sticky shreds of
lettuce, and the tongue (which, in fact, is descended from the same cells
in the embryo that split off to make the sexual organs). I notice her open
mouth, her pink throat, and I dangerously lift a foot and lean.

• • •

Homage

In a marble stall
of the third floor bathroom
at the University of Pittsburgh,
on the wall to your right
as you're sitting, a woman
has written (with a black marker)
lines of a poem by Lucille Clifton—
> come celebrate
> with me that everyday
> something has tried to kill me
> and has failed
—either copied from a book
or remembered by heart,
written with a firm,
defiant hand.
Once Lucille
packed a tent at Dodge
with 20,000 people.
Here she has
an audience
of one, the pee
spilling out, the bowels
with their steamy stink. A slave
might leave such a message
in a secret place
to point the way
North. To every woman
who lowers herself,
pass it on.

Jerry Stern's friendship

He's cracked a vertebra
& can barely move; &
when I call to check,
we get to talking about
the time I came to Iowa.
We've been friends since
before he published his first book,
before I wrote mine. I was luckier
than the beauties that men
loved to lay,
then bullied after—
I was tongue-tied
around the ones I wanted. But Jerry,
even though testosterone haloed him
like incandescent hula hoops—a light
that made me mad & envious!—
was one from whom I never felt
a spark of murderous heat.
I listened for hours,
for years, to the mind
that remembered everything;
passion that flowed (not as rage,
but as outrage) like honey
from the great hive-
heart of God &, slowly,
trusted. He's 93—writing
more than ever!—& confesses that
that night, when I stayed
in his upstairs guestroom,
he stood on the landing
turned on as he watched me
climb his old farmhouse stairs.

La fille aux cheveux de lin

It hurts me to lift
the old record from its
paper cover, to bring Walter Gieseking
to life again. The needle
is heavy with pain, and yet it bumps
down lightly, releasing
the sumptuous, thread-fine
brightness pressed
into vinyl
when the great pianist
played for the Nazis. On the cover,
his eyes are soulless, as dull
as one who has given over
his true gift
to the devil. The notes
fly above
the crematoriums—*sorrow*
you name, sorrow
you are part of—
"The girl with the flaxen hair."

Lauds

Good morning, fat chair. Your frame is slight-
Ly askew, your wooden bones tilt, but padded
With foam & polka-dotted, you seem sprite-

Ly, good-natured. I've known a chair to rise
Out of a night's darkness & provide a ride
For me, above the furry carpeting, defy-

Ing gravity. Even one cock-eyed, cheap,
Can be a tilted ship climb-
Ing waves of mourning. Whatever light

Shines through this morning's slatted blinds—
Smoky with undelivered rain—I've turned aside
To praise my last-legged you, for (like Jessie

Norman's lungs) your soul breathes blithe
Operatic air, & your polka dots climb
Atmospheric strophes like poems I memorized

In school. Do not go gentle, fat chair. What we write
About we are, so you are me, plumped with an extra
Twenty pounds, a bear, lumbering. But, in a poem, we
Dance with a relic of imagination &, by imagination, live.

Midnight: Long Train Passing

The steady growl of it, not rattling
the windows, but continuous, like
white noise. I sit in a huge armchair,
hoping it will
go on forever; for,
when I was a child
awake and fearful, I'd hear the whistle
and rumble of a far-off train
and be comforted,
as if it were another person, another body,
and I was, suddenly,
inside it, its heartbeat
trembling through the wood. It seemed
to cover me, like the sheet
I'd pull over my head
so that nothing
could crawl in my ear.
It was a language
that carried me, so that
all the hours, days, and years I
thought I was unworthy, I was not. Instead
there was another self I lived in, like a God
I prayed to by staying alive.

My father in old age

My father enjoyed
such innocent pleasures
at the end, his face
unguarded as a
three-year-old's—bacon
with tomato on a slice
of thickly buttered toast.
He'd look up and make
sounds from deep
in his belly, MMMMM-
UMPHFFF, he'd sing, extending it, holding
on to the MMMMMs, then letting them go
with a quick staccato. When my father
was young, no matter how hard
he beat me, his face never
unclenched itself. His hardest work
never helped him. Then,
at the end,
an unrehearsed joy . . .

A nap

Alone in my house
during a rainstorm
I open the back door so that the
sound comes in &
rain makes a little puddle
inside the screen It is
early afternoon, though dark,
I lie on the bed
& put my papers down beside me I am
light, as if there were no
blame or guilt—light
inside, heavy out—each part
of me balanced, supported.

New Orleans palmetto bug

We . . . feel a kiss on our lips
Trembling there like a small insect.
ARTHUR RIMBAUD

1. False Gods

I'm terrified of the one
in my kitchen. It's as long as my index finger,
& two thumbs wide—so big, so
alive with its bigness, that I can't imagine
putting my foot on top & pressing—
any more than I could imagine
pressing down
on a hummingbird or newborn kitten.
I'm screaming &
waving my hands, but it doesn't move. Then, slow
& steady, it starts to walk toward me. I'm yelling,
"You dumb ass, you stupid mother fucker." I'm so
big, so
powerful, I can't believe
it won't
obey me! "Ok," I say, this time
with assurance, "You better not
go in my bedroom," but it does the very thing
I told it not
to do, heads straight
down the hall, through my door & climbs up
on the heater
beside my bed. (Imagine
me trying to sleep & feeling
that slight tremble
on my lips!) I grab the heater

& carry it, carefully (I don't want to hurt
it when it falls!), out the front door
to the porch, begging, "Please, go home
to your own people." But it holds on,
as if it doesn't want to leave.

Later, as I'm drifting off,
I hear the long soft clickings
of a chorus
outside my window & I wonder
if it has brought back
a bunch of its friends
to serenade me to sleep.

2. Why the giant palmetto bugs in New Orleans run toward you when you are screaming at them to go away

They have a hard thing
on the top of their head that sticks out
like the bill of a baseball cap (but pointy),
so they can't
look up; they
only see the ground & don't know
you're screaming & waving
your hands. They see only
your foot & they imagine
its cool shadow: what a good place
to hide, they say.

Note

If the slaves
could create gospel
music & praise

God, then, Toi,

no
more
grumbling!

Pantoum for the Broken

How many of us were fingered?
A soft thing with a hole in it,
a thing that won't tell, that can't.
I forget how many times I was broken,

a soft thing with a hole in it.
Some remember, grateful it wasn't worse;
I forget how many times I was broken.
Someone faceless rolled on me like a horse.

Some remember, grateful it wasn't worse.
Some forget but their bodies do inexplicable things.
Someone faceless rolled on me like a horse.
Sleepwalking, I go back to where it happens.

Some forget but their bodies do inexplicable things.
We don't know when or why or who broke in.
Sleepwalking, we go back to where it happens.
Not wanting to go back, we make it happen.

If we escaped, will we escape again?
I leapt from my body like a burning thing.
Not wanting to go back, I make it happen
until I hold the broken one, hold her and sing.

The Peaches of August

The long-awaited, here, at the local farm stand, are not as comely as
the ones at Whole Foods, but they are dollars cheaper, and so we sweep
them up like sweepstakes winners, and stack them in our purposeful
cloth bags. Tomorrow, one of us, before the other awakens, will slice
into Tupperware the 4 or 5 softest to the fingers (to test, press kindly as
a newborn's cheek), and stir them with brown sugar from a box atop
the refrigerator.

The permission

I don't care. Write anything you want about me.
It's not about me, anyway. Whatever you write, it's about you.
                                        BRUCE DERRICOTTE

There is a language that says
size doesn't matter. It's supposed to help

us who can't do better. But we must
do better.

Something

changed & so

we tried harder.
We used unnatural devices

We made hay

• • •

Imagine a plastic
cup over a wavering

penis. How could hardness

not save us? How could we, then, not
make it, force it,

if need be?

We mustn't cry   mustn't give up: the spectacle

of a man with an angel
strapped to his thigh

that keeps coming

loose

• • •

The wife still wants it.

Meat   Meat   Meat on a
spindle or a salty plate not tears

but the labia puffed &
sweet. I have no will to let go

of what I long for:
a last drive

• • •

Is poetry meant to handle

the inner sanctum, the blasted

bed? It would help
if it were somebody else's

business

to confess, to lay bare an
embarrassment. Let him have a dead

man's pride. But I am willing

to breathe life in   to take

it in my hands

•   •   •

I always thought
we wouldn't have to come to

what shouldn't have to be tried because
we shouldn't have come to this

•   •   •

We succumbed
to the evening news

tongue-tied   old lovers

for whom there was one
sad language

& too much riding
on that piece

The proof

After thirty years, I was done
with talking. I had told him

I was leaving, but still we'd sit
at the dinner table—me to his right—& I'd watch him. He'd

put the forkfuls in his mouth & chew,
a calm look on his face. How I wanted him

to suffer, to see that there was some

register where it
mattered. If he would just turn

his eye, like a great
planet, slowly, as if over

epochs. I wouldn't have left

if he had
looked at me with

sorrow or, perhaps, not even
sorrow, but turned toward me with sudden

awareness. Why were tears

pouring down my
cheeks? It wasn't that he was angry,

that would have been
a kind of recognition. If anything confirmed

my going, it was that
absence—not even cool—as if there was nothing

between us that couldn't be dissolved
by will; nothing that could be

altered by desire.

He would often tell me about a tree
in his childhood that was right in the middle of a

baseball field, a huge old tree
where the kids played ball, so that they had to

run around it to hit second base, how the coaches
wanted to take it down . . . but there was one old man who fought

for the tree &, though he didn't win & the tree was cut, whenever
Bruce went home, years later, there was a perfect

field but nobody ever played
there. Is the mystery that no matter what I felt

was missing, there is something
that remains? But he went on, the meat

chewed, the water in the glass
swallowed. Perhaps what I had put on the table tasted

good, perhaps he was appreciating
my efforts, that I had called him, that, as usual, I had

made dinner for us. Perhaps he was concentrating
on something I couldn't see—me, so determined

to affect him, to make him pay. Wasn't there a right

& a wrong here? I remember the time I decided

to move to Pittsburgh
for the job, to stay married but to live

apart. We had gone out to
the Frank Lloyd Wright house, Fallingwater,

& we sat by the stream. He confessed
that something in him had been missing

all those years. He talked about his
childhood—the fears, of him being

the only black
boy in that town, & how his mother brought the news

of lynchings fifty miles away
in Indiana & taught him not to touch

the white girls
who flirted. He didn't present it

to change anything, not for

sympathy but, as it happened, sometimes—if rarely
in our 30 years together—that

we showed ourselves without even a scintilla
of the will

to make things better. & that's what made it so

terrible & blinding, so
true.

Rereading Jerry Stern

I realize that I no longer want to write perfectly constructed and "deeply meaningful" poems. I see what a great gift it is if a writer just truthfully records the way her mind moves: seizing on one thing, one connection, and running with it like a cat might run behind an unwinding ball, wherever it goes—down the back stairs (which, today, for some reason, seem to be dusted with years of unswept flour!), unrolling down a hall and into a back bedroom (though why was that particular door ajar?).

Sex in old age

Are we a-
sexual now, touching
each other tenderly, more
tenderly than a mother,
the dear, dear
body in our hands? You touch me
as if each cell of you remembers
where I live. I live
here and here, everywhere
you touch moves, as if a breath
is passing over baby hairs.
Your hand passing
down my back, cupping
my buttocks, I can't remember
in between,
my body is lost in your
making, my mind
asking, *what is this quick*
parting of dead cells, this
brushing away
of small planets?
You are too naked
to take in, like the whole
David, O

nipple of light
on my tongue.

Streaming

What do you do
with the time in which
you no longer worry,
no longer undoing
every little victory
as if it were a knot?
I laze about streaming
a hundred and nine episodes
of "Brothers and Sisters" waiting
for the seventy-year-old uncle
to admit he's gay, and the mother,
The Flying Nun, as old as I
am and grounded, to stop
looking for love in
all the wrong places and grab
a poem out of the air—
the way Ruth Stone said she took
no credit, just
thought of the universe
and stuck her hand up in it
like a baseball mitt.

Summer evening at Still Point

the centre cannot hold . . .
WILLIAM BUTLER YEATS,
"The Second Coming"

In the middle of fixing dinner,
like ducklings follow the mother duck,
we follow Sister Sylvia to the spring-fed pond.
At first, reluctant; and then, exultant,
until every one of us belly flops in
in our clothes. The water's delightful, a little cooler
than the summer air, and so clear green, you can
keep your eyes open without stinging.
The "gift" ducks (Sylvia's recent hustle
from the local farm), fuss and scatter
as she ploughs the center and turns
face up to heaven. Though her rice is burning!
And it's twenty minutes past the dinner bell.

Telly redux: Sharon asks me to
send a picture of little fishie Telly

Love is memory lit.

I wish I had
taken his picture but,

in those days, some part of my heart was still
unswimmingly

cold &, as much as I loved

Telly, I couldn't imagine
carrying a fish's

picture in my wallet, or
putting one (in a gold frame)

on the same mahogany
shelf with my grandson. All I have today

is
the Telly in my heart, a shimmery

thinking
in red veils. I remember

his swishy tail, a magisterial emblem

of the Living God. In heaven we will swim together

through clouds & spheres of wonder
far beyond

this unpardoning
glass of water.

Watching a roach give birth on YouTube,
I think of Lucille Clifton meeting God

When I watch it push out
the purse (half

the size of its own body) that contains

a hundred jelly-
like nymphs, a labor that takes a molasses-

slow twenty-four hours—I wonder

is it—she!—
like us—pushing

with all she's got? Or is hers a

painless birth, like we like to think

of the Virgin Mary's, without
a smear

of shit or blood? Why does God

make every damn
female

have to work

so hard & suffer? Lucille, even after

breast cancer, even after her

kidneys failed & the twice weekly

dialysis, didn't get really
mad at God until her youngest

girl, Fredericka,

died of a brain tumor
at 35. Then she didn't speak

to God

for years. Not until her granddaughter

Bailey was born
did she give thanks

again, saying

that part of her lost
daughter had returned. How she loved

& praised it all. Toward the end,
she told me she wasn't

angry at God anymore, but that,

when she got to heaven,
she had some

very tough questions
for him. Once Lucille visited

a grade school in Maryland
where, walking through the library, she noticed

a distinct
lack of color

on the shelves. Where are the books

with black
children in them, she asked. The assured

librarian had a swift
reply: "We don't have any

black children in this school, so we don't need
those books," she said. "Well, you don't

have any
bunnies in this school either, but you seem to have

plenty of books

about bunnies."
                              Poor God, I thought, who,

having made
her shining brain—our brilliant Morning

Star—must have seen

Her coming.

"What are you?"

My DNA tells the same story as my face—
The mix that makes me at home in Greek,

Italian, Spanish, and Portuguese restaurants.
My skin duskier to sensors trained—

The sniffing nose, the prickly skin,
Ears alert for loud laughter, for the *coloreds'* speech that,

Now, almost seventy years after desegregation, so often
Tricks, so that, when the actual person arrives

Who called about that house for sale, the agent stutters:
That property has just been sold. My answer changes.

For years, to avoid conversations that would take
A lifetime, minds purposely dulled for generations

("Single consciousness," Dubois might have called it),
I would say when introduced—to avoid later embarrassment

For us both—*I'm Toi Derricotte, I'm black*, and stick my hand out.

Now—is it pride in our complexity, and having written proof
From Ancestry.com that makes me sputter on about how

My ancestors (perhaps theirs too?) freighted cargo
Around the Mediterranean to places not yet named and bordered—

Genetic free-for-alls? *Humans and Neanderthals had sex and produced*
Viable offspring—but most evidence places these encounters in the Middle East,

Just after early humans exited Africa some 50,000–60,000 years ago.

Recently, caught in conversation at a cocktail party, I quoted
Percentages to curious whites: 72 percent European, 28 African

(A blend which, in New Orleans, in the 17th and 18th centuries,
Wouldn't have bought a ticket to the Quadroon Ball!). Their faces

Waited for the punch line, until the black woman I was with cracked
The silence: *You've been black all your life*, she answered everyone.

To our various shades, another friend made it perfectly
Clear fifty years ago: *If you black you black.*

• • •

What changed when white people first saw (were amazed—
As they are now—the first time) a black person? In European

Towns in World War II, they wanted to touch the skin, the hair—
Black soldiers became accustomed to it on the streets where children

Wanted to put their hand in it, press it, smiling
In disbelief, gawking at features,

Putting their arms and hands against
The color to check, entranced, as if they'd discovered another planet.

Think of Keats and Chapman's Homer:
Then felt I like some watcher of the skies
When a new planet swims into his ken;
Or like stout Cortez when with eagle eyes
He star'd at the Pacific — and all his men
Look'd at each other with a wild surmise —

Silent, upon a peak in Darien.

I wonder if Richard Wilbur was awakened
By the browns and blacks of *our* skin before he could awaken

To "the beautiful" in his famous poem:
The beautiful changes as a forest is changed
By a chameleon's tuning his skin to it;
As a mantis, arranged
On a green leaf, grows
Into it, makes the leaf leafier, and proves
Any greenness is deeper than anyone knows.   For surely,

Any blackness is deeper than anyone knows. Or Tiffany's
Idea, in 1885, to make glass's colors more vibrant, "Their rich tones

Are due in part to the use of pot metal full of impurities." Slavery
A generation gone, and my great-grandmother, Philomene,

Still a Louisiana washwoman with her fifty daily pounds
Of white women's dirty laundry on her head.

●　●　●

I've seen
A toddler flinch on the elevator at an entering face, don't

Touch, we are all trained in what not to see. Everywhere
In the world. I know an unnamed (forgotten, unspeakable) cemetery
Where the unwanted
Half-breed babies were swaddled tight and abandoned without funeral
Marker or blessing. *What are you?* A question black people
Never ask, perhaps, catching the drift of a slave ship

In my speech, most likely, what I laugh at
Or how I laugh, for the first laughter surely erupted from the deepest
Cavern, from Olduvai Gorge (*praise Lucy who, in Ethiopia, is also known as Dinkinesh,*
"You are marvelous" in the Amharic language).
Each wavelength of a chuckle is a measurable rift
Between the consciousness of those without and those with
Ownership of their bodies.

My ancestors, before there were lines
Of hatred and difference drawn around parcels
Of ground, landed on the circle of the beaches of the
Mediterranean, in Europe or Africa, so that my mother's nose was
"Aquiline," my skin color would find family
In any city. What makes me black?
That thin strip of DNA across
The middle of the continent that shuttled us to the Ivory Coast,
All our DNA is marked by it, the same
Red flag, the magic carpet-ride through Ghana
To the sea, no matter
Where the other dots on the map reside—Ireland, England, Finland—
No matter how far fetched, what makes me black is a splash of color
Through the map, a swath, a gash, an epoch of four hundred years
Of blood, semen, and vomit that poured out through Cape Coast,
and from that wound the bloody tears dispersed.

The Empress of the Death House

• • •

sleeping with mr. death

when you have hung the keys on the wall
& all you are left with is
mr. death
you untie his shoelaces
& roll him in
he is the shoulder you rub
on a cold night
he is the breath
you attend to
put your hand on his belly
& feel the stone bowels
he moves in the morning
measure the width
of his African nose
calculate the number of deaths
in his penis

you go down on him
he bursts in yr mouth
a thousand stars
flicker, then die

chalk-dry, mr. death

in the breeze from an open window
his bones
clatter like music

the story of a very broken lady

I.

the babies i have not been able to have
the slippery rubbery dolls
that have not been able to squeak through my thighs

i am splintery   i guard me like glass

i am old as dry kindling
i go up like an attic
belching my black smoke & fire

i must have praise
i must have praise like Our Lady

a light
must fall
on the ton
in my belly

No little ones to crack through my pelvis.
No little ones to crack me in two.

in my mother i choked on the cord
the out-going breath
struggled & caught

my voice snapped like a neck

so i make no music
i am jealous of my time
i tire like an old lady

they take me to the top of the stairs
remove my white shift
& stroke between my legs
to get the clear urine.

i am thirsty   i itch like a monk's suit

II.

my house has become a secret
my children no longer speak to me
when i come home
they pass through me like ghosts

they are silent of comfort
they address me with the same respect
as dead ancestors

they turn away from me
like death in the future

i keep company under the hills
with scarves & with feathers
my O mouth for howling

nothing but crumbs & but slumber

my house is unfurnished
it is common as Howard Johnson's

it is the outside i turn to
windows
framing the view
like a woman's mahogany hair

nobody hears me
i talk & i talk

the walls close over me
my mother buries me
in the sound of her cooing

my father my doctor comes
bowing at my frightful pinkness
i am hot as pain
he keeps his hands off

he clucks like pigeons
he parades like fat roosters
he eats me like eggs

the bones of my tongue crack
on the roof of his mouth.

old troll lady,

old blankets & feathers
wave from my hole in the hill
wave my wild scarves
while the hole of my mouth
grows darker
& my speech is a sound
of no color

the mirror poems

Je vous livre le secret des secrets.
Les miroirs sont les portes par
lesquelles la Mort va et vient.

COCTEAU

Prologue:

If she could only break the glass—
the silver is already peeled back like first skin
leaving a thin
transparent thing that floats across the ground
in front of her : this white shadow.

1. what a mirror thinks

a mirror thinks it has no self
so it wants to be everything it sees

it also thinks everything is flat

put a bunch together
& they think they see
the back side of the moon

2. the mirror as a judge of character

keening my appetite
on the taste of an image of myself
sharpening myself
on bones;
suddenly
i lean over its eye
& see the way i see myself

i ask it
am i fairest in all the land

it opens like a backwards lake
& throws out of its center
a woman
combing her hair
with the fingers of the dead

3. the mirror & suicide

someday
stand before a mirror & feel
you are drowned

let your hair spread
as sweet Ophelia's did
& you will rock
back & forth
gently
like a boat in kind water

4. questions to ask a mirror

remember:
whatever you ask a mirror
it will ask back

if you ask it
what will you give me
it will ask you
what will you give me

if you ask it what is love
it will turn into a telescope
& point at you

if you ask it what is hate
it will do the same thing

if you ask it what is truth
it will break in nine pieces

if you ask it what is beauty
it will cast no reflection

if you ask it to show you the world
it will show you the eye of your mother

5. <u>conversing with the mirror</u>

never tell a mirror you are black
it will see you as a rainbow
never tell a mirror you are white
it will make you disappear
in fact a mirror doesn't care
what color you are

never tell a mirror
how old you are
under 20
you draw a blank
over 40 it stares

never cry in front of a mirror
it gets cruel

if a mirror doesn't trust you
it squints

if a mirror hates you
it speaks in a high-pitched voice

if a mirror calls you long distance
don't accept the charges hang up

never run from a mirror
it always leaves a friend outside

never have sex with a mirror
you will have in-grown children

don't take money from a mirror
there are strings

if you must converse with a mirror
say to it: you're pretty
& won't get broken

that gives you
7 years

6. the mirror & time

the mirror IS NOT immortal
in fact it only has nine lives:

the first one is a thief
the second a baker
the third plays the harpsichord

the fourth lives in the iron-bound
section of newark &
eats pork sausage
the fifth predictably drinks
the sixth goes into the convent
but the seventh (this gets better)
marries her father
& humps up like a camel
the eight cries a lot and ZAP
changes into a writer

7. the mirror & metamorphosis

the eye   in the mirror   is the mirror   of the eye

8. the mirror & the new math

inside the mirror
opens up like the number zero
you swim around in there
bob up
or drown
like the rat in Wonderland's flood.

your tail would like to hook a reason,

but you keep coming
face to face
breast to breast
with yourself.

you fall backwards & away, even
think that you are lost

in Oceanic O,

but you are still
pinned to an inverse.

9. the mirror as a silent partner

the mirror never talks
it is always astounded
with its O mouth open
& everything falling in

Epilogue:

Always straining toward her image, the girl
let go.

Tentacles of light
unlocked
like hooks of parasite

& she came back
in dark so dark,

she cannot see by sight

the face/as it must be/of love

i touch your nose
& what beneath

the flesh mat
thick & soft
the brain grey as goat's curd
the kind cup of your skull

when will i break this mirror of your eye

in it

the moon
drags the water
on the shadow of its back

the earth
dims
like a jewel in darkness

& my face
hangs, starless
as dime-store crystal

doll poem

doll is sitting in a box
she watches me
with 2 grey eyes
i take the top off
& look at her
she is wearing rubbers
to keep her feet dry
she is wearing eyeglasses
2 inches thick
she has padding on her soft behind
she is wearing excuses
all over
she is carrying threads
& buttons
she is good hausfrau
prepared for all necessities
with kleenex
& kotex
& pencils
& lifesavers
& a boy doll with a wedding ring
she has lists as endless as dirt
      a grocery list
      a Xmas list
      a wine list
      a list of sins
      a list of movies
      a list of friends
her lists grow up
& eat lbs. of other lists

she is clean clean clean
she is rabbit quick
she copulates with ideas
she is good as gold
she is desirable as a tooth-fairy
she is the color of permanent
teeth
ask her her name
and turn her over
she says, ma ma

new lady godiva

she stops at the gas station
goes into the john &
unzips

her epidermis

peels out of it
skillfully
as a prostitute

long strips
slip to the pee-wet floor
& melt

like cotton candy

thus baptized
& pink as veal,

she goes to meet the public.

The Grandmother Poems

The Empress of the Death House

My mother, bastarded by southern
greed; the rammed, inseparable
seed dyeing her cells,
married north.
I recall the weekly
visits to my grandmother's,
Webster's Funeral Home,
where we courted a northern
mother who hadn't yet put thumbs
up on any name but "Mrs. Webster."

Wednesdays, pinafored, packed
in blue velvet leggings from Saks
Fifth, we pegged the snow-long
blocks of Detroit's striving
colored Conant Gardens
to a last-ditch bus line
where we waited hours,
hopping back and forth on ice-
licked feet in a night of white
more blind than any other.

And sometimes, joking
about the red-striped mechanical
beast who slept remorseless
in his heated stall, we
turned and tunneled
home.

Though I was only five,
and mother never said a word,
I wondered why

my grandmother,
green-eyed, henna-haired,
Empress of the Death House,
never launched her ship,
the Fleetwood, laying course
for far off Conant Gardens
where these cold survivors,
her inheritors,
waited clench-jawed, brass-clean
to perform their weekly rabbit scene.

The Feeding

My grandmother
haunted the halls
above Webster's Funeral
Home like a red-
gowned ghost. Til dawn
I'd see her spectral
form—henna-hair
blown back,
green eyes:
tameless.

She was proud.
Like God,
I swore I'd love her.
At night we whispered
how we hated mother
and wished that I could
live with *her*.

In the morning while she slept,
I'd pluck
costume diamonds
from a heart-shaped chest,
try her tortoise combs
and hairpins in my hair.
She'd wake
and take me to her bed.

Maroon-quilted, eider-downed,
I drowned.
Rocking on her wasted breast,
I'd hear her tell me
how she nursed my father
til he was old enough to ask.

Then she'd draw me
to her—ask me
if she still had milk.
Yes. I said, yes.
Feeding on the sapless
lie, even now
the taste of emptiness
weights my mouth.

The Funeral Parade

Over the Ambassador Bridge—
an arc of perpetual pregnancy—

we ride
to bury the dead.

Leading the way is one
blind, deaf, dumb:

the path has been cut,
we are doing our duty.

Grandfather,
in spats.

Grandmother,
tailor-made.

& the small child, the mourner,
blind as the buried.

from a group of poems thinking about
Anne Sexton on the anniversary of her death

> *Look, you con man, make a living*
> *out of your death.*
>
> HEMINGWAY

Questions for Anne

Did your poems write you like nightmares:

Did they play "shuffle-off-to-Buffalo" like the Ames Bros.:

Did they dry up like Whaleback Waddy:

One night, did you come home
to toast your toes in front of them
& did they leave you cold:

Did they leave you in the lurch
like a teenaged poppa:

Anne,

We are your children,

Where is the note, explaining. . . .

Answers from Anne

yes.   my poems dreamed me like nightmares—

yes.   they ended me like a cheap novel—

yes.   they played music on my backbones. fish butchers.

        i was their ankh, their xylophone
        they owned me "Z" to "A"

        THEY were the artist

        i was the whore   the canvas

        i was ivory keys—
        their beast of 5 fingers

but when the time came, nothing could stop me, i tell you:

i made a living of my death

unburying the bird

buried birds
are usually
dead.
fallen from the sky
because of too much
something.
        too much high.
        too much steep.
        too much long.
        too much deep.
but sometimes
one has been known
to go underground.
you do not hear a peep
for years.
then one day,
you go back to the spot
thinking you will not find
a feather or a few
scattered bones
& you hear something
pecking   trying
to get out of there.
you are afraid to believe
it is still alive.
afraid that even if it is
in being freed, it will die.
still,
slowly,
you go about freeing the bird.
you scrape away the grave

which in some mysterious way
has not suffocated her.
you free her scrawny head,
her dangling wing.
you keep thinking her body
must be broken beyond healing.
you keep thinking the delicate
instruments of flight
will never pull again,
still,
you free her.
feed her from the tip of your finger.
teach her the cup of your hand.
you breathe on her.
one day,
you open up your hand
& show her sky.

Natural Birth

• • •

Introduction

Writing *Natural Birth*

I wrote *Natural Birth* when my son was sixteen years old.

I had told no one of the story of his birth in a home for unwed mothers, not even my best friend, and especially not my son.

What if my baby knew I was such an imperfect mother? That he wasn't wanted from the moment he was conceived, that he hadn't been planned for, that it was not like a Hallmark card? For much of my pregnancy I had felt nothing but shame, guilt, anger, and depression. At the birth I felt numb, disconnected. If my son knew, would he feel unloved, unworthy? Would he feel it was his fault?

By showing one woman's experience, which so diverged from the ideal, which I believe does testify to the power of nature and love, I hoped to revise the ideas of a painless "natural birth"—birth without the use of drugs—that had been published in the fifties and sixties. I wanted *my* natural birth to hold on to the mystery and power of that singular rite of passage, at the same time that it stripped away the romantic and ideal. I wanted to imply that every creative act, whether it is giving birth to a child, a work of art, or the self, is unique, arduous, and awe-full.

please, god, make it easy,
i said it would be easy.
i don't want a shot. i
want it to be beautiful
like it's supposed to be . . .

In my seventh month, I traveled to a maternity home in another city. When I arrived, there was no room until December. I was placed with the Reynolds family until space was available.

november

nun meets me at the station. first month with carol and
dick reynolds. *set the table. clean the kitchen. vacuum.
thank god she didn't ask me to take care of the children.*

i dry dishes in the afternoon. watch her can apples from
the backyard, put them in the cellar dark to save for winter.

*why is everything so quiet? why does the man come home
from school everyday at 3:30 and read the paper? why a
different casserole on the table every night and everyone
eats one portion and one portion only? why is there always
enough, but never too much . . .*

try to understand this quiet, busy woman. is she content?
what are her reasons to can, to cook, to have three children
and a pregnant girl in her house? try to be close, lie
next to their quiet ticking bedroom and hear no sound,
night after night, except soft conversation. in the morning,
before light, i hear the baby's first cry. i picture her
in there with her bra unhooked and her heavy white breast
like cream on the cheek of that baby.

inside i wonder what she thinks, feels, who she is. and
every night it gets dark earlier, stays dark later. i don't
want to wake up smiling at cereal. dark overshadows snow,
and a fear comes into my cold heart: *i am alone.*

one afternoon, drying dishes, her cutting apples by the
sink, i ask her about college. i picture her so easily
in penny loafers, peck and peck collar, socks, and a plaid
skirt on her skinny still unchilded body. here she is today

with hips and breasts, a woman thirty who had taught school—
she must have some thoughts, some arguments and passions
hidden in this kitchen.

finally, she tells me her favorite book is *the stranger*.
we go and find it on the living room shelf. i wonder,
though she never says, what she understands about
being a stranger.

i meet her mother. all the same—they treat me all
the same: human. i am accepted, never question who
i am or why. never make me feel unwanted or afraid.
but always human love and never passion, never clutching
need, lopsided devouring want, never, not one minute,
extending those boundaries to enclose me . . .

                            oh soul,

                                   i feel

cold and unused to such space as breath and eternity
around me.
        so much room in silence . . .

how will *my* house ever run on silence, when in me there
is such noise, such hatred for peeling apples, canning,
and waking to feed baby, and alarm clocks in the soul, and
in the skin of baby, in the rind of oranges, apples, peels
in the garbage, and paper saved because it is cheaper to
save and wrap and wash and use everything again. and clean,
no screaming in that house, no tears, one helping at dinner,
and no lovemaking noises like broken squeaky beds. where is
that part i cannot touch no matter where or how i tum,
that part that wants to cry: *SISTER*, and make us touch . . .

she is kind. though i never understand such kindness.
cannot understand the inner heart of how and why she
loves: *i am the stranger*.

somewhere in the back of my mind, they are either fools
or the holy family, the way we all should be if we lived
in a perfect world and didn't have to strive to be loved,
but went about our quiet business, never raising our voices,
never questioning if we are loved, or
whether what we do is what we want to do, or worth it.

and if they are fools who don't have hearts or brains
or cords in their necks to speak, then why have they
asked for me? why am i in their house? why are they
doing this?

one night in my round black coat and leotards, i dress
up warm against the constellations, go down the snowy
block alone in time. i am only going to the drugstore,
but for some reason, the way i feel, pregnantly beautiful
walking into the bright fluorescent drugstore, it is
the most vivid night in my mind in the whole darkening
november.

In my ninth month, I entered a maternity ward set up for the care of unwed girls and women in Holy Cross Hospital.

holy cross hospital

couldn't stand to see these new young faces, these
children swollen as myself. my roommate, snotty,
bragging about how she didn't give a damn about the
kid and was going back to her boyfriend and be a
cheerleader in high school. *could we ever "go back"?*
would our bodies be the same? could we hide among the
childless? she always reminded me of a lady at the bridge
club in her mother's shoes, playing her mother's hand.

i tried to get along, be silent, stay in my own corner.
i only had a month to go—too short to get to know them.
but being drawn to the room down the hall, the t.v. room
where, at night, we sat in our cuddly cotton robes and
fleece-lined slippers—like college freshmen, joking
about the nuns and laughing about due dates—jailbirds
waiting to be sprung.

one girl, taller and older, twenty-six or twenty-seven, kept
to herself, talked with a funny accent. the pain on her face
seemed worse than ours . . .

and a lovely, gentle girl with flat small bones. the
great round hump seemed to carry *her* around! she never
said an unkind word to anyone, went to church every morning
with her rosary and prayed each night alone in her room.

she was seventeen, diabetic, fearful that she or the baby
or both would die in childbirth. she wanted the baby, yet
knew that to keep it would be wrong. but what if the child
did live? what if she gave it up and could never have another?

i couldn't believe the fear, the knowledge she had of
death walking with her. i never felt stronger, eating
right, doing my exercises. i was holding on to the core,
the center of strength; death seemed remote, i could not
imagine it walking in our midst, death in the midst of
all that blooming. she seemed sincere, but maybe she
was lying . . .

she went down two weeks late. induced. she had decided
to keep the baby. the night i went down, she had just
gone into labor so the girls had two of us to cheer about.

the next morning when i awoke, i went to see her. she
smiled from her hospital bed with tubes in her arms. it
had been a boy. her baby was dead in the womb for two
weeks. i remembered she had complained *no kicking*. we
had reassured her everything was fine.

meanwhile i worked in the laundry, folded the hospital
fresh sheets flat three hours a day. but never alone.
stepping off the elevator, going up, feeling something,
a spark catch. i would put my hand there and smile with
such a luminous smile, the whole world must be happy.

or out with those crazy girls, those teenagers, laughing,
on a christmas shopping spree, free (the only day they
let us out in two months), feet wet and cold from snow.

i felt pretty, body wide and still in black beatnik
leotards, washed out at night. my shapely legs and
young body like iron.

i ate well, wanted lamaze (painless childbirth)—i
didn't need a husband or a trained doctor—i'd do it
myself, book propped open on the floor, puffing and
counting while all the sixteen-year-old unwed children
smiled like i was crazy.

one day i got a letter from my cousin, said:

don't give your baby up—
you'll never be complete again
you'll always worry where and how it is

she knew! the people in my family knew! nobody died
of grief and shame!

i *would* keep the child. i was sturdy. would be a better
mother than my mother. i would still be a doctor,
study, finish school at night. when the time came, i
would not hurt like all those women who screamed and
took drugs. i would squat down and deliver just like the
peasants in the field, shift my baby to my back, and
continue.

when my water broke, when i saw that stain of pink blood
on the toilet paper and felt the first thing i could not
feel, had no control of, dripping down my leg, i heard
them singing mitch miller xmas songs and came from the
bathroom in my own pink song—down the long hall, down
the long moment when no one knew but me. it was time.

all the girls were cheering when i went downstairs. i was
the one who told them to be tough, to stop believing

in their mother's pain, that poison. our minds were
like telescopes looking through fear. it wouldn't hurt
like we'd been told. birth was beautiful if we believed
that it was beautiful and right and good!

maternity—i had never seen inside those doors.
all night i pictured the girls up there, at first hanging
out of the windows, trying to get a glimpse of me . . .
when the pain was worst, i thought of their sleeping faces,
like the shining faces of children in the nursery. i held
onto that image of innocence like one light in the darkness.

pain is as common as flies. if you don't see it
walking on your lip, if you can't breathe it,
don't feel it for yourself, you walk in darkness.
not knowing the price of common sunshine,
air, the common footstep on the earth. one
moment of life must be paid for, and no one
walking in the darkness without eyes can see.

the child is cut off from the mother, cut off
from the blinding pain the mother sleeps
and wakes up in forever, balancing the asshole
of the universe, the abyss of god's brain, inside
that light in her forehead.

she is bright. so bright that everything must
turn and face her like the sun. every clock
in life must stop to let her pass. slowly,
like the regal death procession of the king.

maternity

when they checked me in, i was thinking: *this is going to be
a snap!* but at the same time, everything looked so different!
this was another world, ordered and white. the night moved
by on wheels.

suddenly the newness of the bed, the room, the quiet,
the hospital gown they put me in, the sheets rolled up
hard and starched and white and everything white except the
clock on the wall in red and black and the nurse's back as
she moved out of the room without speaking, everything
conspired to make me feel afraid.

how long, how much will i suffer?

the night looked in from bottomless windows.

going to the bathroom. worse than cramps. can't stop
going to the bathroom. shaking my head over the toilet.
just sit. sit on the toilet. don't move. just shake
your head. try to go so hard. maybe it will go away.
just try. press real hard. *it hurts i can't help it oh
it hurts so bad!*

lie on the bed and can't breathe right. go to sleep and
wake up in the middle of a wave, too late . . .

what time is it, i can't keep track of time . . .

fall asleep. two minutes. can't stand the pain. have
to go to the bathroom. feels so ugly pressing down there,
shame, shame! have to go to the bathroom all the time.
shake my head. can't believe it hurts like this and
getting worse.

lie back in bed, just breathe. just relax. watch the
clock. one minute goes so slow. seems like 10:29—the
clock is stuck there, stuck on pain . . .

nurse comes in, asks me if i want a shot. *no i don't want a
shot. i want this to be easy. please god make it easy, i said it
would be easy. no i don't want a shot don't want to give up
yet, i want it to be beautiful like it's supposed to be if i just
breathe right, can't give up they want me to give up i won't
give up* (the minutes stuck around the clock), *please
nobody see me* (the nurse says the social worker wants to
see me . . . and the social worker is pregnant!) *god don't
let her see. i told her to have lamaze like me told her it was*

easy and not to be afraid. don't let her see how hard don't let her be afraid like i am now. never again, never have a baby, never believe that this is beautiful or right or good i'm rolling in the dark the clock is stuck the big black clock is stuck all night. inside i'm quiet outside i roll and can't stop it getting worse, can't stop it's getting worse—it can't get worse! how could a body hold such pain? how could such pain be here and how and what did i do? i want to scream i can't. my mouth is stopped my mouth is dry— so dry god let me out of this hell i did my exercises loved my baby did everything i could, you promised if i was good you promised if i was clean and pure and beautiful, if i was humble like a child and loved them all the little children (so far the bathroom, so cold in the night loving my baby, so far, so cold, so long) *and no one to come and save me from this pain i cannot stop oh god no one to save me . . .*

i watch the clock. 10:29. wait, desperate to see
time go. it all depends on time. everything depends
on those black lines on the clock. the second hand
goes round. i want to push it, pray it into place.
between each second are millions of seconds that must
be touched and passed. the clock goes nowhere. or
else i look again, and it has gone back.

*time is going nowhere only me inside of time is getting
deeper getting lost can't skate across the hours forgetting
memory of pain no where to hide each moment is a desert
i must cross can't find the sides of anything everything
expanding growing wider larger only me inside of time is
growing smaller disappearing in a wider hole of nothing
i have never been alive before, never want to be alive again . . .*

doctor comes in, wrenches his hand, a hammer up my cunt.
wants to feel the head, wants to feel the damn thing's
head, wants to see how far i am. and i roll and moan
and beg him not to see, but he keeps "seeing." (no
pain like this ever.) and i am thinking, *this is the one*
who told me i would hurt. FORGET ALL THAT SILLY
BREATHING STUFF. YOU'LL TAKE A SHOT LIKE THE
REST WHEN THE TIME COMES. now, every time he
sticks that wooden board up me, jams that stake inside my
bleeding heart, i know, this is one who likes to give me pain.

this is static. no stop between. how can they know the
mountain of pain in me? how can every woman suffer so?
how can every man and woman walking on legs, the thousands
you see each day, how can each have had a mother like me?
how can life contain it? how can any woman know and let
this happen? one pain like this should be enough to save
the world forever.

the nurse says she'll give me a shot. still wants to
give me a shot. *but i don't want a shot. i've tried so hard*
all night to stay awake and fight and breathe, and now it's
8:00 and might go on like this forever i want to be awake
and see my baby, want to see him crown, the head immense
as sun and bright with blood crack over the bowl of earth i
want to feel the womb of god close over me, and want to,
more than anything, feel joy and love and welcome him god
help this man be born into this world help his mother wants
to share this moment with his beauty wants to hold on to
the pain a second more and feel him crown inside me majesty
and might no more than being humble will allow a broken
woman, let me be awake and push him into light . . .

it's light outside it's light i can see it in the mirror
day is coming night is passing i am so far in myself
i can't see out can't say no to anything floating on my
pain . . .

doctor comes in to feel the head. keeps coming in,
making me hurt, sticking his whole hand up my asshole.
and it hurts like sticking a wooden ax handle up my cunt
and grinding it inside me, hot cigars burning ax handles
and i can't move i'm in such pain, can't move away from
him raping me each time sticking his whole gloved hand
up my wounded cunt.

my heart is open. my whole body is open and cannot say
no. my mouth, each mouth inside me is open and bleeding.
each heart is like the moon without a middle, a white
hole in the sky so wide the sun has gone through.

he must be happy to make me feel such pain. he must be
happy because he is a man and in control of me and i
cannot move away from him while he takes me on this bed
of pain and he tells me it is for my own good when i
tell him how i hurt, he tells me it is almost over, but
the clock is stuck on pain, stuck on forever, and i know
that he is lying.

he wants me to roll and beg like a dog, *please doctor*
please don't hurt me anymore do anything do anything you
say but help me help me not to feel such pain but i don't
beg him. i don't beg him because i hate him. i keep
my pain locked up inside. he'll never know how much
he hurts me, i'll never let him know.

my heart is frozen like a calf. on ice. my heart is
empty meat. my heart, my love is frozen. i will never
love again.

up there. the girls are in the dark. behind
dark panes of glass. i cannot look in, but
i can see their faces. they are happy for me.
they have gone to sleep with smiles on their
faces. they are happy because i have
gone down.

but i am so alone.

tonight all windows are gray and shuttered
by paper. all rooms are closed to me tonight
except this room, awash with brightness.

far away, across the courtyard, up through
darkness, like the dark around a ship without
a thought of land, is light, another light, the
light of girls' dreams.

how i wish that one would light a candle,
all night a candle of consciousness lit
outside my pain. but i am far away, lost to
the sight of land, and they are quiet, like
children in the nursery.

let them sleep tonight, ignorant of where i
stand (their knowledge cannot help). but how
will i ever look beauty in the face again,
once blinded by this light?

transition

the meat rolls up and moans on the damp table.
my body is a piece of cotton over another
woman's body. some other woman, all muscle and nerve, is
tearing apart and opening under me.

i move with her like skin, not able to do anything else,
i am just watching her, not able to believe what her
body can do, what it *will* do, to get this thing accomplished.

this muscle of a lady, this crazy ocean in my teacup.
she moves the pillars of the sky. i am stretched into
fragments, tissue paper thin. the light shines through
to her goatness, her blood-thick heart that thuds like
one drum in the universe emptying its stars.

she is
that heart
larger
than my life
stuffed
in
me
like sausage

black sky
bird
pecking
at the bloody
ligament

trying

to get
in, get
out
i am

holding out with
everything i
have
holding out
the evil thing

when i see there is
no answer
to the screamed
word
GOD
nothing i can do,
no use,

i have to let her in,
open the door,
put down the mat
welcome her
as if she
might be the
called-for death,
the final
abstraction.

she comes.
like a tunnel
fast
coming into

blackness
with my headlights
off

you can push . . .

i hung there. still hurting, not knowing what to do.
if you push too early, it hurts more. i called the
doctor back again. *are you sure i can push? are you sure?*

i couldn't believe that pain was over, that the punishment
was enough, that the wave, the huge blue mind i
was living inside, was receding. i had forgotten there
ever was a life without pain, a moment when pain wasn't
absolute as air.

why weren't the nurses and doctors rushing toward me?
why weren't they wrapping me in white? white for respect,
white for triumph, white for the white light i was being
accepted into after death? why was it so simple as saying
you can push? why were they walking away from me into
other rooms as if this were not the end the beginning of
something which the world should watch?
i felt something pulling me inside, a soft call, but i
could feel her power. something inside me i could go
with, wide and deep and wonderful. the more i gave
to her, the more she answered me. i held this conversation
in myself like a love that never stops. i pushed toward
her, she came toward me, gently, softly, sucking like a
wave. i pushed deeper and she swelled wider, darker when
she saw i wasn't afraid. then i saw the darker glory
of her under me.

why wasn't the room bursting with lilies? why was
everything the same with them moving so slowly as if
they were drugged? why were they acting the same when,
suddenly, everything had changed?

we were through with pain, would never suffer in our
lives again. put pain down like a rag, unzipper skin,
step out of our dead bodies, and leave them on the
floor. glorious sprits were rising, blanched with
light, like thirsty women shining with their thirst.

i felt myself rise up with all the dead, climb out of
the tomb like christ, holy and wise, transfigured with
the knowledge of the tomb inside my brain, holding the
gold key to the dark stamped inside my genes, never to
be forgotten . . .

it was time. it was really time. this baby would be
born. it would really happen. this wasn't just a
trick to leave me in hell forever. like all the other
babies, babies of women lined up in rooms along the halls,
semi-conscious, moaning, breathing, alone with or without
husbands, there was a natural end to it that i was going
to live to see! soon i would believe in something larger
than pain, a purpose and an end. i had lived through to
another mind, a total revolution of the stars, and had
come out on the other side!

one can only imagine the shifting of the universe, the
layers of shale and rock and sky torturing against each
other, the tension, the sudden letting go. the pivot of
one woman stuck in the socket, flesh and bones giving

way, the v-groin locked, vise thigh, and the sudden release when everything comes to rest on new pillars.

where is the woman who left home one night at 10 p.m.
while everyone was watching the mitch miller xmas show?
lost to you, to herself, to everyone

they finished watching the news, went to sleep,
dreamed, woke up, pissed, brushed their teeth, ate
corn flakes, combed their hair, and on the way out
of the door, they got a phone call . . .

while they slept the whole universe had changed.

delivery

i was in the delivery room, PUT YOUR
FEET UP IN THE STIRRUPS, i put them up, obedient,
still humbled, though the spirit was growing larger
in me that black woman was in my throat, her thin
song, high pitched like a lark, and all the muscles
were starting to constrict around her.
i tried to push just a little. it
didn't hurt. i tried a little more.

ROLL UP, guzzo said. he wanted to give me
a spinal. NO. I DON'T WANT A SPINAL. (same
doctor as ax handle up my butt, same as shaft
of split wood, doctor spike, driving the
head home where my soft animal cowed and prayed and
cried for his mother.)

or was the baby
part of this
whole damn
conspiracy,
in on it with
guzzo,
the two of them
wanting to shoot
the wood
up me for
nothing,
for playing
music to him
in the dark
for singing

to my round
clasped
belly
for filling
up with
pizza on a cold
night, dough
warm.

maybe
he
wanted
out,
was saying
give her
a needle
and let me/the hell/
out of here
who cares
what she
wants
put her
to sleep.

           (my baby
           pushing off
           with his black
           feet
           from the dark
           shore, heading
           out, not
           knowing
           which way and trusting,

oarless and eyeless, so
hopeless
it didn't matter.)

no. not
my baby.
this
loved
thing
in/and of
myself

so i balled up
and let him
try to
stick it in.
        maybe
something was
wrong.

       ROLL UP
he said
       ROLL UP
but i don't want it
       ROLL UP ROLL UP
but it doesn't hurt

we all stood,
nurses, round the white
light
hands
hanging
empty at our sides

ROLL UP IN A BALL

all of us not
knowing
how
or if
in such a world without
false promises
we could say
anything
but, *yes,*
yes.
come take it
and be quick.

i put my belly in my hand
gave him that
thin side
of my back
the bones
intruding on the air
in little knobs
in joints
he might
crack
down my spine
his knuckles
rap
each twisted
symmetry
put me on
the rack,
each
nerve

bright
and stretched
like canvas.

he couldn't get it in!
three times, he tried
ROLL UP, he cried, ROLL UP
three times
he couldn't get it in!

dr. y (the head obstetrician)
came in

"what are you
doing, guzzo,
i thought she
wanted
natural . . .

(to me) *do*
you want
a shot . . . no? well,

PUT YOUR LEGS UP,
GIRL, AND
PUSH!"

and suddenly, the light
went out
the nurses
laughed
and nothing
mattered

in this 10
a.m. sun
shiny morning
we were well
the nurses and the
doctors cheering
that girl
combing hair
all in one
direction
shining
bright as water.

        i
grew deep
in me
like fist and i
grew deep
in me
like death
        and i
grew deep
in me
like hiding in the sea and
i was
over me
like
sun and i
was under
me
like sky and i
could look
into myself

like one
dark eye.

    i was her
and she was me
and we were
scattered round
like light
      nurses
      doctors
cheering

              such waves

my face
contorted,
never
wore
such mask, so
rigid
and so dark

     so
bright, un-
compromising
brave
no turning
back/no
no's.

i was so

beautiful. i
could look
up in the
light and
see my huge-
ness,
arc,
electric,
heavy, fleshy, living
light.

no wonder they
praised me,
a gesture
one makes
helpless and
urgent, praising
what goes on
without our praise.

when there
was nowhere
i could go, when i
was so deep
in myself
so large
i had to
let it out
they said
      drop back. i
dropped back
on the table
panting,

they moved
the head, swiveled
it correctly

        but i

                i

was
losing
her. something
        a head
coming through
the door.
NAME PLEASE/
PLEASE/NAME/whose

head/i
don't know/some/
        disconnection

                NAME PLEASE/

and i
am not ready:

the sudden visibility—
his body,
his curly wet hair,
his arms
abandoned in that air,
an arching, squiggling thing,
his skin must be

so cold,
but there is nothing
i can do
to warm him,
his body clutches
in a wretched
spineless way.

they expect me
to sing
joy   joy
a son is born,
child is given.
tongue
curled in my head
tears, cheeks
stringy with
damp hair.

this lump
of flesh,
lump of steamy
viscera.

       who

is this
child

       who

is his father

a child
never having
been seen
before,
without
credentials
credit cards without
employee
reference or
high school grades or
anything
to make him
human make
him mine but
skein of
pain to
chop off
at the navel.

while they could
they held him down and
chopped him, held him up
my little fish, my blueness
swallowed in the air
turned pink
and wailed.

no more. enough.
i lay back, speechless, looking
for something.

to say to myself.

after you have
touched the brain,
that squirmy
lust of maggots,
after you have
pumped the heart,
that thief,
that comic, you
throw her in the trash.

and the little one
in a case
of glass . . .

> *he is not i*
> *i am not him*
> *he is not i*

. . . the stranger.

blue
air
protects us from each other.

here.
here is the note he brings.
it says, *mother*.

but i do not even know
this man.

in knowledge of young boys

i knew you before you had a mother,
when you were newtlike, swimming,
a horrible brain in water.
i knew you when your connections
belonged only to yourself,
when you had no history
to hook on to,
barnacle,
when you had no sustenance of metal
when you had no boat to travel
when you stayed in the same
place, treading the question;
i knew you when you were all
eyes and a cocktail,
blank as the sky of a mind,
a root, neither ground nor placental;
not yet
red with the cut nor astonished
by pain, one terrible eye
open in the center of your head
to night, turning, and the stars
blinked like a cat. we swam
in the last trickle of champagne
before we knew breastmilk—we
shared the night of the closet,
the parasitic
closing on our thumbprint,
we were smudged in a yellow book.

son, we were oak without
mouth, uncut, we were
brave before memory.

Captivity

• • •

But even when I am at a loss to define
the essence of freedom
I know full well the meaning
of captivity.

ADAM ZAGAJEWSKI
(Translated by Antony Graham)

The Minks

In the backyard of our house on Norwood,
there were five hundred steel cages lined up,
each with a wooden box
roofed with tar paper;
inside, two stories, with straw
for a bed. Sometimes the minks would pace
back and forth wildly, looking for a way out;
or else they'd hide in their wooden houses, even when
we'd put the offering of raw horse meat on their trays, as if
they knew they were beautiful
and wanted to deprive us.
In spring the placid kits
drank with glazed eyes.
Sometimes the mothers would go mad
and snap their necks.
My uncle would lift the roof like a god
who might lift our roof, look down on us
and take us out to safety.
Sometimes one would escape.
He would go down on his hands and knees,
aiming a flashlight like
a bullet of light, hoping to catch
the orange gold of its eyes.
He wore huge boots, gloves
so thick their little teeth couldn't bite through.
"They're wild," he'd say. "Never trust them."
Each afternoon when I put the scoop of raw meat rich
with eggs and vitamins on their trays,
I'd call to each a greeting.
Their small thin faces would follow as if slightly curious.
In fall they went out in a van, returning

sorted, matched, their skins hanging down on huge metal
hangers, pinned by their mouths.
My uncle would take them out when company came
and drape them over his arm—the sweetest cargo.
He'd blow down the pelts softly
and the hairs would part for his breath
and show the shining underlife which, like
the shining of the soul, gives us each
character and beauty.

Blackbottom

When relatives came from out of town,
we would drive down to Blackbottom,
drive slowly down the congested main streets
    —Beubian and Hastings—
trapped in the mesh of Saturday night.
Freshly escaped, black middle class,
we snickered, and were proud;
the louder the streets, the prouder.
We laughed at the bright clothes of a prostitute,
a man sitting on a curb with a bottle in his hand.
We smelled barbecue cooking in dented washtubs,
    and our mouths watered.
As much as we wanted it we couldn't take the chance.

Rhythm and blues came from the windows, the throaty voice of
    a woman lost in the bass, in the drums, in the dirty down
    and out, the grind.
"I love to see a funeral, then I know it ain't mine."
We rolled our windows down so that the waves rolled over us
    like blood.
We hoped to pass invisibly, knowing on Monday we would
    return safely to our jobs, the post office and classroom.
We wanted our sufferings to be offered up as tender meat,
and our triumphs to be belted out in raucous song.
We had lost our voice in the suburbs, in Conant Gardens,
    where each brick house delineated a fence of silence;
we had lost the right to sing in the street and damn creation.

We returned to wash our hands of them,
to smell them
whose very existence
tore us down to the human.

Christmas Eve: My Mother Dressing

My mother was not impressed with her beauty;
once a year she put it on like a costume,
plaited her black hair, slick as cornsilk, down past her hips,
in one rope-thick braid, turned it, carefully, hand over hand,
and fixed it at the nape of her neck, stiff and elegant as a crown,
with tortoise pins, like huge insects,
some belonging to her dead mother,
some to my living grandmother.
Sitting on the stool at the mirror,
she applied a peachy foundation that seemed to hold her down,
    to trap her,
as if we never would have noticed what flew among us unless
    it was weighted and bound in its mask.
Vaseline shined her eyebrows,
mascara blackened her lashes until they swept down like feathers,
darkening our thoughts of her.
Her eyes deepened until they shone from far away.

Now I remember her hands, her poor hands, which even then
    were old from scrubbing,
whiter on the inside than they should have been,
and hard, the first joints of her fingers, little fattened pads,
the nails filed to sharp points like old-fashioned ink pens,
    painted a jolly color.
Her hands stood next to her face and wanted to be put away,
    prayed
for the scrub bucket and brush to make them useful.
And, as I write, I forget the years I watched her
pluck hairs like a witch from her chin, magnify
every blotch—as if acid were thrown from the inside.

But once a year my mother
rose in her white silk slip,
not the slave of the house, the woman,
took the ironed dress from the hanger—
allowing me to stand on the bed, so that
my face looked directly into her face,
and hold the garment away from her
as she pulled it down.

St. Peter Claver

Every town with black Catholics has a St. Peter Claver's.
My first was nursery school.
Miss Maturin made us fold our towels in a regulation square
    and nap on army cots.
No mother questioned; no child sassed.
In blue pleated skirts, pants, and white shirts,
we stood in line to use the open toilets
and conserved light by walking in darkness.
Unsmiling, mostly light-skinned, we were the children of the
    middle class, preparing to take our parents' places in a
    world that would demand we fold our hands and wait.
They said it was good for us, the bowl of soup, its
    pasty whiteness;
I learned to swallow and distrust my senses.

On holy cards St. Peter's face is olive-toned, his hair
    near kinky;
I thought he was one of us who pass between the rich and poor,
    the light and dark.
Now I read he was "a Spanish Jesuit priest who labored for
    the salvation of the African Negroes and the abolition
    of the slave trade."
I was tricked again, robbed of my patron,
and left with a debt to another white man.

The Weakness

That time my grandmother dragged me
through the perfume aisles at Saks, she held me up
by my arm, hissing, "Stand up,"
through clenched teeth, her eyes
bright as a dog's
cornered in the light.
She said it over and over,
as if she were Jesus,
and I were dead. She had been
solid as a tree,
a fur around her neck, a
light-skinned matron whose car was parked, who walked
    on swirling
marble and passed through
brass openings—in 1945.
There was not even a black
elevator operator at Saks.
The saleswoman had brought velvet
leggings to lace me in, and cooed,
as if in the service of all grandmothers.
My grandmother had smiled, but not
hungrily, not like my mother
who hated them, but wanted to please,
and they had smiled back, as if
they were wearing wooden collars.
When my legs gave out, my grandmother
dragged me up and held me like God
holds saints by the
roots of the hair. I begged her
to believe I couldn't help it. Stumbling,
her face white

with sweat, she pushed me through the crowd, rushing
away from those eyes
that saw through
her clothes, under
her skin, all the way down
to the transparent
genes confessing.

Fires in Childhood

I. Aerial Photographs Before the Atomic Bomb

Why did such terrible events
catch my eye? After Hiroshima,
I turned the picture in *Life* around
in circles, trying to figure out this huge
wheel in the middle of the air, how it
turned, a Ferris wheel, its lights
burning like eyes.
The atom spinning
on course over the sleeping,
vulnerable planet. I turned it the way one might
turn a kaleidoscope or prism. Even then I
knew about the town lying under,
like a child sleeping under the
watchful gaze of a rapist, before the spasm
of stopped breath, the closure at the
scream of the throat, before the body is awakened
along its shocked spine to bursting
light, the legs closing, the arms,
like a chilled flower. That eye, that spinning eye

seeking the combustible.
This was a heat
I had felt already in our house on Norwood.
                                             Everything
looked green, placid as a green field,
predictable as machinery—an antique clock.
This was the instant
before destruction,
the fiery atom stuck

as if under the control of the artist
before it spilled and became irretrievable.
Could it be sucked back
in its lead bag, the doors of the underbelly slammed,
and those men who went on to
suicide and madness, go on instead
to become lovers, priests, Buddhist
smilers and scholars, gardeners in the small plots
of contained passion?

II. The Chicago Streetcar Fire

... burning out of the
center of the *Free Press*, its peeling paint
crackling like paper.
I hid the pictures from my mother, needing to see
those who were fried in an
iron skillet, the men, women, children
melted together in a crust of skin,
a blackened hand more dense
than charred steak, as if it had been
forgotten in the fire years. They crammed together
at the exit as if terror could
leap through locked doors.
Only a fraction of an inch
from safety! Maybe if one had
gone the other way—
blood going up in flames
like gasoline, heads torches.
Children who did not
escape their childhoods—

Feathers!   Ash!

High School

I didn't want to be
bunched with the black girls in the back
of Girls Catholic Central's cafeteria.
They were my kin,
but sitting there I was aware
of that invisible wall, the others
circling us like stars. The others:

Gintare,
the Ukrainian with limbs like silk and childbearing hips.
Kathleen, who would be a nun, whose mother saw the Virgin in
the suburbs.
Pignalls, whose body had grown into a giant's, who towered
over the gold prom queens, not like a man, but a child who
had grown into a monster, her broken speech a path out of
herself she could not follow.
Donna, her hair hanging over her face like a veil—her knees
made for kneeling, her stomach for fasts, her genitals for
the loneliness of the cot, but the rest of her unable to hold
up holiness.
Jo, who let boys penetrate and shrugged off other wisdoms;
her long eyelashes held grains of sand, as if tiny pieces of
eternity were working themselves through her.
Lenore, whose square body threatened the narrow pews;
expelled, who lived in the back of a White Tower with her
first woman lover.
Marty, whose palate and teeth stuck out, like some hairy
specimen of our ancestors, alone with her mother, sleeping
on the pull-out cot.

None of them called me nigger;
but they were ignorant
as God of our suffering.

Hamtramck: The Polish Women

What happens to the beautiful girls with slender hips and
  bright round dresses?
One day they disappear without leaving a trace of themselves,
and the next they appear again, dragging a heavy
  shopping cart from the bakery to the pork store with
  packages of greasy sausage and potatoes.
Like old nuns they waddle down the main street, past the rich
  gaudy cathedral with the little infant of Prague—in
  real clothes—linens they tend lovingly, starch in
  steamy buckets (their hands thick as potatoes, white),
  and iron with dignity.

The Struggle

We didn't want to be white—or did we?
What did we want?
In two bedrooms, side by side,
four adults, two children.
My aunt and uncle left before light.
My father went to the factory, then the cleaners.
My mother vacuumed, ironed, cooked,
pasted war coupons. In the afternoon
she typed stencils at the metal kitchen table.
I crawled under pulling on her skirt.
What did we want?
As the furniture became modern, the carpet deep, the white
ballerina on the mantel lifted her arms like some girl near
terror;
the Degas ballerinas folded softly in a group, a gray sensual
beauty.
What did we push ourselves out of ourselves
to do? Our hands
on the doors, cooking utensils, keys; our hands
folding the paper money, tearing the paid bills.

Before Making Love

I move my hands over your face,
closing my eyes, as if blind;
the cheek bones, broadly spaced,
the wide thick nostrils of the African,
the forehead whose bones push
at both sides as if the horns
of new-fallen angels lie just under,
the chin that juts forward with pride.
I think of the delicate skull of the Taung child—
earliest of human beings
emerged from darkness—whose geometry
brings word of a small town of dignity
that all the bloody kingdoms rest on.

[The Taung child is a fossil, a juvenile
Australopithecus africanus, from Taung,
South Africa, two million years old.]

On Stopping Late in the Afternoon for Steamed Dumplings

The restaurant is empty
except for the cooks and waiters.
One makes a pillow of linens
and sleeps, putting his feet up in a booth;
another folds paper tablecloths. Why
have I stopped to eat alone on this rainy
day? Why savor the wet meat of the
steamed dumpling? As I pick it up,
the waiter appraises me. Am I
one of those women who must stop
for treats along the way—am I that starved?
The white dough burns—much too hot—yet,
I stick it in my mouth, quickly,
as if to destroy the evidence.
The waiter still watches. Suddenly
I am sorry to be here, sad,
my little pleasure stolen.

Stuck

The traffic backs up.
We're not moving.
The CB says it's construction
on the bridge. "I should be driving," I say.
"I'm afraid to be stuck on a bridge."
"It's only a short one," you say,
"just over the Connecticut River."
I sit back on my backbone.
"Shouldn't you be in that lane? It
  seems to be moving faster." "Yeah,
  but the CB says the left lane
  is open on the bridge."
We sit. The truckers are angry—
"Another four-wheeler messin' things up."
The four-wheelers are angry—
"Goddamn eighteen-wheelers fuckin' up the bridge."
The right lane moves ahead.
My heart pounds;
  my palms glaze with sweat.
If I were driving, I say to myself, I'd
move into that fast lane, then
cut back in front of the others. You are
calm, humming, tapping the steering
wheel with your fingers—though the car
in front of us is letting drivers
cut back in.
"No cuts," I want to scream.
  But I keep silent, count
  my breaths to thirteen
  and start again.

Squeaky Bed

At your mother's house we lie
stiff in our bed as paper dolls.
Soon you snore and the crickets burst
through the window with squeaky horns.

She is old and toothless,
when we make love we
rock in the arms of a
new mother, she will not hear.

The crickets never sleep. All night
they want it.
Love is more real
than fear. Soon we will
give ourselves over to the noise.

The Good Old Dog

I will lay down my silk robe
beside me near the old bed,
for the good old dog;
               she loves the feel
of it under her, and she will
push it and pull it, knead
and scrape until she has it right;
               then she'll drop down,
heavy, silver and black in the moonlight,
on it and a couple of pillows (not
bothering the cat who has taken over
               her real bed)
                        and breathe out deeply.

Gorgeously fat,
her face
like the face of a seal.

The Promise

I will never again
expect too much of you. I have
found out the secret of marriage:
I must keep seeing your beauty
like a stranger's, like the face
of a young girl passing on a train
whose moment of knowing illumines
it—a golden letter in a book.
I will look at you in such
exaggerated moments, lengthening
one second and shrinking eternity
until they fit together like man and wife.
My pain is expectation:
I watch you for hours sleeping, expecting
you to roll over like a dead man,
and look me in the eye;
my days are seconds of waiting
like the seconds between the makings
of boiling earth and sweating rivers.
What am I waiting for if not
your face—like a fish floating
up to the surface, a known
but forgotten expression that
suddenly appears—or like myself,
in a strip of mirror, when, having
passed, I come back to that image
hoping to find the woman
missing. Why do you think I sleep
in the other room, planets away,
in a darkness where I could die solitary,
an old nun wrapped in clean white sheets?

Because of lies I sucked
in my mother's milk, because
of pictures in my first grade reader—
families in solid towns as if
the world were rooted and grew down
holding to the rocks, eternally;
because of rings in jewelers' windows
engraved with sentiments—*I love you
forever*—as if we could survive
any beauty for longer than just after . . .
So I hobble down a hall
of disappointments past where
your darkness and my darkness have
had intercourse with each other.
Why have I wasted my life
in anger, thinking I could have more
than what is glimpsed in recognitions?
I will let go, as we must
let go of an angel called
back to heaven; I will not hold
her glittering robe, but let it
drift above me until I see
the last shred of evidence.

For a Man Who Speaks with Birds

Always, around the others
you wear your body
as if you put on the old
football pads of boyhood;
they are still much too large for you,
you turn and twist in them
like a man in the sheets of a nightmare.
Businessmen choose you to lead them,
you step forward
built for defenses—barreled ribs
around the heart of one
who wants to speak to the redbirds.
Are you trying to find a way out,
like a woman stuck between floors
pushing all the dead buttons?
Your mouth has spoken
the whistles of redbirds,
but your eyes know how to look
from a great height,
as a king must have watched
a slave from a window.

I pity you going from town to town
with your satchel of orders
from devil to devil;
your bones must hold up such metal
while your heart wants to speak
in the tongues of red angels.

Touching/Not Touching: My Mother

i.

That first night in the hotel bedroom,
when the lights go out,
she is already sleeping (that woman who has always
claimed sleeplessness), inside her quiet breathing
like a long red gown. How can she
sleep? My heart beats as if I am alone,
for the first time, with a lover or a beast.
Will I hate her drooping mouth,
her old woman rattle? Once I nearly
suffocated on her breast. Now I can almost
touch the other side of my life.

ii.

Undressing
in the dark,
looking,
not looking,
we parade before each other,
old proud peacocks, in our stretch marks
with hanging butts. We are equals. No
more do I need to wear her high heels to step
inside the body of a woman.
Her beauty and strangeness no longer seduce
me out of myself. I show my good side, my
long back, strong mean legs, my thinness that
came from learning to hold back
from taking what's not mine. No more
a thief for love. She takes off her

bra, facing me, and I see those gorgeous
globes, soft, creamy,
high; my mouth waters.
how will I resist
crawling in beside her, putting
my hand for warmth under
her thin night dress?

My Father Still Sleeping after Surgery

In spite of himself,
my father loved me. In spite
of the hands that beat me, in spite
of the mouth that kept silent, in spite
of the face that turned cruel
as a gold Chinese king,
he could not control the love
that came out of him.
The body is monumental, a colossus
through which he breathes.
His hands crawl over his stomach
jerkily as sand crabs on five legs;
he makes a fist
like the fist of a newborn.

Boy at the Paterson Falls

I am thinking of that boy who bragged about the day he threw
    a dog over and watched it struggle to stay upright all
    the way down.
I am thinking of that rotting carcass on the rocks,
and the child with such power he could call to a helpless
    thing as if he were its friend, capture it, and think of
    the cruelest punishment.
It must have answered some need, some silent screaming in a
    closet, a motherless call when night came crashing;
it must have satisfied, for he seemed joyful, proud, as if he
    had once made a great creation out of murder.
That body on the rocks, its sharp angles, slowly took the shape of
    what was underneath, bones pounded, until it lay on the bottom
    like a scraggly rug.
Nothing remains but memory—and the suffering of those who
    would walk into the soft hands of a killer for a crumb of bread.

Fears of the Eighth Grade

When I ask what things they fear,
their arms raise like soldiers volunteering for battle:
Fear of going into a dark room, my murderer is waiting.
Fear of taking a shower, someone will stab me.
Fear of being kidnapped, raped.
Fear of dying in war.
When I ask how many fear this,
all the children raise their hands.

I think of this little box of consecrated land,
the bombs somewhere else,
the dead children in their mothers' arms,
women crying at the gates of the bamboo palace.

How thin the veneer!
The paper towels, napkins, toilet paper—everything
burned up in a day.

These children see the city after Armageddon.
The demons stand visible in the air
between their friends talking.
They see fire in a spring day
the instant before conflagration.
They feel blood through closed faucets,
the dead rising from the boiling seas.

The Furious Boy

In the classroom, the furious boy—a heavy star.
The unhappiness in the room finds his heart,
                enters it;
The sheet of paper flapping in his face.
Who takes something takes it from him.

The rejections look for him.
The inflicted pain finds him.
He cannot say no. The hole in his heart deepens,
pain has no way out. A light too heavy
to escape, a presence more concentrated,
warmth is everywhere except where he sits at the center
holding the world in place.
The children touch him gently; the teacher lets him be.
                                Such a weight!
One black child in a perfect town;
there is no reason for sadness.

In an Urban School

The guard picks dead leaves from plants.
The sign over the table reads:
Do not take or *touch* anything on this table!
In the lunchroom the cook picks up in her dishcloth
what she refers to as "a little friend,"
shakes it out,
and puts the dishcloth back on the drain.
The teacher says she needs stronger tranquilizers.
Sweat rises on the bone of her nose,
on the plates of her skull under unpressed hair.
"First graders, put your heads down. I'm taking names
so I can tell your parents
which children do not obey their teacher."
Raheim's father was stabbed last week.
Germaine's mother, a junkie,
was found dead in an empty lot.

The Polishers of Brass

I am thinking of the men who polish brass in Georgetown;
bent over, their hands push back and forth with enormous
    force on each square inch.
So many doors, knobs, rails!
Men in their twenties, men in their sixties;
when they have gone all around and arrive at the place
    where they started, it has already tarnished, and they must
    begin again.

For the Dishwasher at Boothman's

I sit in front of him
and look him in the eye.
Pastrami on rye.

So accustomed to being invisible,
he startles, as if a door
opened and revealed his face.

His smile says, you should know better,
and he nods his head to the right
like a low angel would nod toward God.

His face is warped
around a center crack, as if
two pains were seamed
together at his birth.

His face would break
his mother's heart.

I read down the left side.
I read down the right.

Plaid Pants

At the bus terminal she says:
"Don't sit next to him,"
and she puts her finger next to her nose
to signal that
one dressed in that garment stinks.

He wears a long white robe,
like a priest with special orders—
the underwear of the Mass—
and a fur cap to cover
his wisdom, so it will stay hot
in this cold climate.
From the soiled seats heading toward Newark,
he stands up. Turning,
I see his face.
I smell nothing, but his face
has its own dark light
inside of the dark
of the cabin, like a moon,
or a candle under smoky glass.
He goes to the bathroom
and comes out a new man—
in plaid polyester pants!

Books

Today Lorca and Pound
fell off my shelf.
They lay there on the floor
like a couple of drunks.
How humble are the lives
of books!
How small their expectations!
They wait quietly,
pressed together,
to be called into
the light. When you open them,
they tell you everything
they know. They
exhaust you with
secrets, like
convicts and madmen
too eager to speak.

Allen Ginsberg

Once Allen Ginsberg stopped to pee at a bookstore
    in New Jersey,
but he looked like a bum—
not like the miracle-laden Christ with electric atom juice,
    not like the one whose brain is a river in which was plunked
    the stone of the world (the one bathing fluid to wash away
    25,000 year half-lives), he was dressed as a bum.
He had wobbled on a pee-heavy bladder
in search of a gas station,
a dime store with a quarter booth,
a Chinese restaurant,
when he came to that grocery store of dreams:
Chunks of Baudelaire's skin
glittered in plastic;
his eyes in sets, innocent
as the unhoused eyes of a butchered cow.
In a dark corner, Rimbaud's
genitals hung like jerky,
and the milk of Whitman's breasts
drifted in a carton, dry as talcum.
He wanted to pee and lay his head
on the cool stacks;
but the clerk took one look
and thought of the buttocks of clean businessmen squatting
    during lunch hour,
the thin flanks of pretty girls buying poetry for school.
Behind her, faintly,
the deodorized bathroom.
She was the one at the gate
protecting civilization.

He turned, walked to the gutter,
unzipped his pants, and peed.
Do you know who that was?
A man in the back came forth.
Soon she was known as
the woman in the store on Main
who said no to Allen Ginsberg;
and she is proud—
so proud she told this story
pointing to the spot outside, as if
still flowed that holy stream.

On the Turning Up of Unidentified Black Female Corpses

Mowing his three acres with a tractor,
a man notices something ahead—a mannequin—
he thinks someone threw it from a car. Closer
he sees it is the body of a black woman.

Medics come and turn her with pitchforks.
Her gaze shoots past him to nothing. Nothing
is explained. How many black women
have been turned up to stare at us blankly,

in weedy fields, off highways,
pushed out in plastic bags,
shot, knifed, unclothed partially, raped,
their wounds sealed with a powdery crust.

Last week on TV, a gruesome face, eyes bloated shut.
No one will say, "She looks like she's sleeping," ropes
of blue-black slashes at the mouth. Does anybody
know this woman? Will anyone come forth? Silence

like a backwave rushes into that field
where, just the week before, four other black girls
had been found. The gritty image hangs in the air
just a few seconds, but it strikes me,

a black woman, there is a question being asked
about my life. How can I
protect myself? Even if I lock my doors,
walk only in the light, someone wants me dead.

Am I wrong to think
if five white women had been stripped,
broken, the sirens would wail until
someone was named?

Is it any wonder I walk over these bodies
pretending they are not mine, that I do not know
the killer, that I am just like any woman—
if not wanted, at least tolerated.

Part of me wants to disappear, to pull
the earth on top of me. Then there is this part
that digs me up with this pen
and turns my sad black face to the light.

A Note on My Son's Face

I.

Tonight, I look, thunderstruck
at the gold head of my grandchild.
Almost asleep, he buries his feet
between my thighs;
his little straw eyes
close in the near dark.
I smell the warmth of his raw
slightly foul breath, the new death
waiting to rot inside him.
Our breaths equalize our heartbeats;
every muscle of the chest uncoils,
the arm bones loosen in the nest
of nerves. I think of the peace
of walking through the house,
pointing to the name of this, the name of that,
an educator of a new man.

Mother. Grandmother. Wise
Snake-woman who will show the way;
Spider-woman whose black tentacles
hold him precious. Or will tear off his head,
her teeth over the little husband,
the small fist clotted in trust at her breast.

This morning, looking at the face of his father,
I remembered how, an infant, his face was too dark,
nose too broad, mouth too wide.
I did not look in that mirror
and see the face that could save me
from my own darkness.

Did he, looking in my eye, see
what I turned from:
my own dark grandmother
bending over gladioli in the field,
her shaking black hand defenseless
at the shining cock of flower?

I wanted that face to die,
to be reborn in the face of a white child.

I wanted the soul to stay the same,
for I loved to death,
to damnation and God-death,
the soul that broke out of me.
I crowed: My Son! My Beautiful!
But when I peeked in the basket,
I saw the face of a black man.

Did I bend over his nose
and straighten it with my fingers
like a vine growing the wrong way?
Did he feel my hand in malice?

Generations we prayed and fucked
for this light child,
the shining god of the second coming;
we bow down in shame
and carry the children of the past
in our wallets, begging forgiveness.

II.

A picture in a book,
a lynching.
The bland faces of men who watch
a Christ go up in flames, smiling,
as if he were a hooked
fish, a felled antelope, some
wild thing tied to boards and burned.
His charring body
gives off light—a halo
burns out of him.
His face scorched featureless;
the hair matted to the scalp
like feathers.
One man stands with his hand on his hip,
another with his arm
slung over the shoulder of a friend,
as if this moment were large enough
to hold affection.

III.

How can we wake
from a dream
we are born into,
that shines around us,
the terrible bright air?

Having awakened,
having seen our own bloody hands,
how can we ask forgiveness,
bring before our children the real
monster of their nightmares?

The worst is true.
Everything you did not want to know.

Tender

• • •

They were all branded, like sheep, with the owners'
marks, of different forms. These were impressed under
their breasts, or on their arms, and, as the mate informed
me, with perfect indifference, "Queimados pelo ferror
quento,—burnt with red-hot iron."

Mr. Walsh, "Notices of Brazil" (1860),
in Rufus W. Clark, *The African Slave Trade*

He shall feed his flock like a shepherd: he shall gather
the lambs with his arm, and carry them in his bosom,
and shall gently lead those that are with young.

Isaiah 40:11

Preface

Tender is not to be read in linear fashion. Rather, it is a seven-spoked wheel, with the poem "Tender" as the hub, each "spoke" or subdivision radiating out from that center.

Violence is central in our lives, a constant and unavoidable reality. Experience is not a linear construct moving from one point to another—childhood to maturity, "bad" to "good," beginning to end—but a wheel turning around a point that shifts between hope and despair.

"At the still point of the turning world," the job of the artist is not to resolve or beautify, but to hold complexities, to see and make clear.

Tender

The tenderest meat
comes from the houses
where you hear the least

squealing. The secret
is to give a little
wine before killing.

Elmina Castle is one of the fortresses in which the slaves were held captive before they were transported across the ocean. Because ships came infrequently and there had to be sufficient numbers of people transported to make a voyage profitable, thousands were often held for months waiting. It is estimated that somewhere between twenty and sixty million Africans were captured, enslaved, and brought to the Americas. The Dutch and Portuguese took slaves from Elmina Castle, a structure built by the Portuguese in 1482, and sent them to Brazil, Surinam, and other colonies. Slaves from Cape Coast, another fortress, were brought to the Caribbean and the United States. Elmina was in operation for more than three centuries.

Exits from Elmina Castle: Cape Coast, Ghana

Gotta make a way out of no way.

TRADITIONAL BLACK FOLK SAYING

The Journey

There is no perfect
past to go back to. Each time I look
into your eyes, I see the long hesitation
of ten thousand years, our mothers' mothers
sitting under the shade trees on boxes, waiting.
There is some great question in your eye that no
longer needs asking: the ball
glistening, wet; the black iris
intense. We know the same things.
What you wait for, I wait for.

The Tour

The castle, always on an
outcrop of indifference;

human shells,
the discards on the way.

Where our mothers were held, we walk now
as tourists, looking for cokes, film, the bathroom.

A few steps beyond the brutalization, we
stand in the sun:
>   *This area for tourists only.*

Our very presence an ironic
point of interest to our guide.

Tourists' Lunch

On a rise, overlooking
the past, we eat
jolaf with pepper sauce and chicken,
laugh, drink beer, fold our dresses
up under us and bathe thigh-
deep in the weary Atlantic.

Beneath Elmina

Down the long, stone ramp,
chained together, unchained finally from the dead,
from months of lightlessness and the imprisoned stink
(a foot-square breech,
the cell's only opening for air—air
which had entered sulfurous, having passed over
the stocks of ammunition),
they pressed and fell against each other.
The only other way (besides death) had been for the few
women who were hauled up into the sun
to be scrutinized by the officers,
the chosen pulled up to apartments
through a trap door:
If they got pregnant, they were set free—
their children becoming the bastard
go-betweens who could speak both tongues.

• • •

At the bottom of the dark stone ramp,
a slit in cement six (?) inches wide,
through which our ancestors were pushed—
the "point of no return,"
so narrow because the Dutch feared
two going together to the anchored ship
might cause rebellion,
and because, starved for so many months,
that opening
was their bodies' perfect fit.

Above Elmina

At the top of the castle,
orderly pews.
We enter under a lintel
carved with news:
This is the house of God.

Slavery

It had struck some of the African Americans
in those dungeons beneath the earth—
though we had come to Africa to heal—there was a huge rip
between us: those were rooms through which *our* ancestors
had passed, while the Africans' had not.
"Another way to look at it," a Nigerian poet answered levelly,
"is that perhaps your ancestors escaped."

Power

The palace of an African king:
two courtyards (a public and a private) in a complex
of bone white stucco edged with a crimson stripe;
the king, in a huge carved chair,
gold-painted and lioned, wearing an understated robe
of grays and browns, his face a structured pleasantness—
the bones of one who has become
slightly more than human;
his ministers smile from faded velvet sofas—
old men with remarkably intact teeth.

A few of us standing in the courtyard
are surprised by a thin man, boyish, though middle-aged,
who comes toward us signaling he is begging—
one hand outstretched, the other nearly touching his lips—
his robe of subtle greens, his feet bare, his naked shoulder
well defined as an aging athlete's. "'The Imbecile Prince,'" our guide explains.
"The only remaining member of the last king's family.
We take care of him as if the present king were his father."

Market

Those huge platters on their heads on which everything
is placed accurately, each small red pepper,
prawn, each orange—arranged in piles so tall they defy gravity—
avocados, crabs, dried fish of silverish brown,
or one great yam, thirty pounds, dirt brushed,
counterbalanced in a kind of aquarium.
A woman approves me with a fluent grin
and offers her light basket for *my* head;
I walk a yard, tottering awkwardly.
The unremarkable commonness—
a beauty shaped by women's hands.

When My Father Was Beating Me

I'd hear my mother in the kitchen preparing dinner. I'd hear the spoons hitting the mixing bowl, the clatter of silver falling into the drawer. I'd hear the pot lids clink and rattle. The normality of the sound was startling; it seemed louder than usual, as if she weren't ashamed, as if she were making a point. Perhaps the house was cut in two by a membrane, and, though her sounds could come to my ears, my screams and cries and whimpers, his demands and humiliations, the sounds of his hands hitting my body, couldn't pierce back the other way. I learned to stretch time and space so I could think what she was thinking. I learned to hear things far away, to live in a thought that could expand itself even until now: What Einstein said is true—everything slows down the farther you get from your mother.

It seemed as if she wanted it, that either I was taking her place, or maybe she thought I deserved it. Maybe there was an overload of violence in the universe, a short in a wire that had to spill its electricity, and she was glad, this time, she hadn't felt it.

Maybe there was some arcane connection between her and my father's hand, his arm let loose and flying, maybe she was in command, making him hit, telling her side of the story—that I was evil, that I had to be beaten, not just for the crime I had committed, but for the crime of who I was: hungry, trying, in every way, to get through barriers set up for my own good. "You're tearing me apart, you're driving me crazy," my mother would scream.

Sometimes I saw the world from her perspective: she *was* beautiful and pitiful and overwhelmed, she was also some blood-sucking witch—not a whole being—able to stretch and contort herself like a cry, something that hated and was flexible. She wanted to beat me in the same way my father did, but she knew she couldn't, because I'd fight back, I'd cry that cry that made her go crazy. "You can't manipulate your father the way you can manipulate me." She meant it as a compliment for herself, as if she loved me more.

They wanted a stillness, a lack of person, place, agony swallowed. They wanted me to die, or, not to die, to exist with a terrible pain, but have it sewn up—as if they could reach into my ribs, crack them open, put a handful of suffering in there and stitch it back, as if my body had a pocket, a black pocket they could stick a thought in that they couldn't stand.

I would fold, collapse like a marionette. (I beat my dolls for years, pounded and pounded and nobody seemed to notice.) "Just keep trying," my father'd say just before he'd strike me. And I did. I kept trying to be beaten.

●　●　●

Serving the dinner plates with her face bland, as if it were virtuous not to take sides, serving the beautiful food that she had cooked all day— her great gift—to say, *I've given everything I could, I've got nothing left.* Often when my father would hit me she'd say, as if he and I were man and wife, "I'm not going to come between the two of you. You two have to work this out for yourselves." He'd give me a warning. "Wipe that look off your face or I'll knock it off. Dry up," he'd scream, "and eat."

Black Boys Play the Classics

The most popular "act" in
Penn Station
is the three black kids in ratty
sneakers & T-shirts playing
two violins and a cello—Brahms.
White men in business suits
have already dug into their pockets
as they pass and they toss in
a dollar or two without stopping.
Brown men in work-soiled khakis
stand with their mouths open,
arms crossed on their bellies
as if they themselves have always
wanted to attempt those bars.
One white boy, three, sits
cross-legged in front of his
idols—in ecstasy—
their slick, dark faces,
their thin, wiry arms,
who must begin to look
like angels!
Why does this trembling
pull us?
A: *Beneath the surface we are one.*
B: *Amazing! I did not think that they could speak this tongue.*

Brother

Jay's mother is brown, mine is white-
looking, as I am, as is our father.
He says sometimes when he'd go
to fill the vending machines
with our father, the white bartenders
would say, "Is that your helper?"
My father would say, "No, he's my
son." Jay says you can always tell
the person changes by something
in the eyes, it may be small—
the eyes open wider or the brow
creases down. He says that once,
our father sent him to get something
from the truck. When he came back,
the bartender had set him up
with a soda, "Have some pop,"
he said in a friendly way. Another time,
when I was doing a reading in New Jersey,
Jay was with me. "A yuppie place,"
he remembers. After the applause
I thanked them and said, "I'd like to
introduce my brother." When he stood
up, people were still looking around
for somebody, looking
right through him. Finally, when they realized
he was *it*, he heard a woman say, "Oh no!"
as if she had been hit in the solar plexus.
Maybe that's why he didn't marry
somebody like us. He married a girl
black as God—and brags to family, strangers,
to *anyone* about that
blackness—so easily recognized, his.

Family Secrets

They told my cousin Rowena not to marry
Calvin—she was too young, just eighteen,
& he was too dark, too too dark, as if he
had been washed in what we wanted
to wipe off our hands. Besides, he didn't come
from a good family. He said he was going
to be a lawyer, but we didn't quite believe.
The night they eloped to the Gotham Hotel,
the whole house whispered—as if we were ashamed
to tell it to ourselves. My aunt and uncle
rushed down to the Gotham to plead —
we couldn't imagine his hands on her!
Families are conceived in many ways.
The night my cousin Calvin lay
down on her, that idol with its gold skin
broke, & many of the gods we loved
in secret were freed.

After a Reading at a Black College

Maybe one day we will have
written about this color thing
until we've solved it. Tonight
when I read my poems about
looking white, the audience strains
forward with their whole colored
bodies—a part of each person praying
that my poems will make sense.
Poems do that sometimes—take
the craziness and salvage some
small clear part of the soul,
and that is why, though frightened,
I don't stop the spirit. After,
though some people come
to speak to me, some
seem to step away,
as if I've hurt them once
too often and they have
no forgiveness left. I feel myself
hurry from person to person, begging.
Hold steady, Harriet Tubman whispers,
Don't flop around.
Oh my people,
sometimes you look at me
with such unwillingness—
as I look at *you*!
I keep trying to prove
I am not what I think you think.

For Black Women Who Are Afraid

A black woman comes up to me at break in the writing
workshop and reads me her poem, but she says she
can't read it out loud because
there's a woman in a car on her way
to work and her hair is blowing in the breeze
and, since her hair is blowing, the woman must be
white, and she shouldn't write about a white woman
whose hair is blowing, because
maybe the black poets will think she wants to be
that woman and be mad at her and say she hates herself,
and maybe they won't let her explain
that she grew up in a white neighborhood
and it's not her fault, it's just what she sees.
But she has to be so careful. I tell her to write
the poem about being afraid to write,
and we stand for a long time like that,
respecting each other's silence.

Passing

A professor invites me to his "Black Lit" class; they're
reading Larson's *Passing*. One of the black
students says, "Sometimes light-skinned blacks
think they can fool other blacks,
but *I* can always tell," looking
right through me.
After I tell them I am black,
I ask the class, "Was I passing
when I was just sitting here,
before I told you?" A white woman
shakes her head desperately, as if
I had deliberately deceived her.
She keeps examining my face,
then turning away
as if she hopes I'll disappear. Why presume
"passing" is based on what I leave out
and not what she fills in?
In one scene in the book, in a restaurant,
she's "passing,"
though no one checked her at the door—
"Hey, you black?"
My father, who looked white,
told me this story: every year
when he'd go to get his driver's license,
the man at the window filling
out the form would ask,
"White or black?" pencil poised, without looking up.
My father wouldn't pass, but he might
use silence to trap a devil.
When he didn't speak, the man

would look up at my father's face.
"What did he write?"
my father quizzed me.

Bookstore

I ask the clerk to show me children's books. I say,
"I'm buying something for my nephew, *Goodnight Moon*.
Are there others you can recommend?" She pulls down
six or seven and I stop her, "Any written by or for black folks?"
She looks as if she doesn't understand. Maybe she has never
heard the words *black folks* before. Maybe she thinks
I'm white and mean it as a put-down. Since I'm white-
looking, I better make it clear. "It's for my brother's son.
'black folks,' black people . . . you know . . . like *me*!"
As quickly as she can, she pulls books from the lower
shelves and loads my arms until the books are falling on the floor.
She wants me to know she's helpful. That her store has so many
to choose from, I couldn't load them in a van. "Thank you, thank you,
that's plenty!" For a moment, history shifts its burden
to *her* shoulders, and the names of the missing are clear.

Invisible Dreams

La poesie vit d'insomnie perpetuelle
RENE CHAR

There's a sickness in me. During
the night I wake up & it's brought

a stain into my mouth, as if
an ocean has risen & left back

a stink on the rocks of my teeth.
I stink. My mouth is ugly, human

stink. A color like rust
is in me. I can't get rid of it.

It rises after I
brush my teeth, a taste

like iron. In the
night, left like a dream,

a caustic light
washes over the insides of me.

• • •

What to do with my arms? They
coil out of my body

like snakes.
They branch & spit.

I want to shake myself
until they fall like withered

roots; until
they bend the right way—

until I fit in them,
or they in me.

I have to lay them down as
carefully as an old wedding dress,

I have to fold them
like the arms of someone dead.

The house is quiet; all
night I struggle. All

because of my arms,
which have no peace!

• • •

I'm a martyr, a girl who's been dead
two thousand years. I turn

on my left side, like one comfortable
after a long, hard death.

The angels look down
tenderly. "She's sleeping," they say

& pass me by. But
all night, I am passing

in & out of my body
on my naked feet.

• • •

I'm awake when I'm sleeping & I'm
sleeping when I'm awake, & no one

knows, not even me, for my eyes
are closed to myself.

I think I am thinking I see
a man beside me, & he thinks

in his sleep that I'm awake
writing. I hear a pen scratch

a paper. There is some idea
I think is clever: I want to

capture myself in a book.

• • •

I have to make a
place for my body in

my body. I'm like a
dog pawing a blanket

on the floor. I have to
turn & twist myself

like a rag until I
can smell myself in myself.

I'm sweating; the water is
pouring out of me

like silver. I put my head
in the crook of my arm

like a brilliant moon.

• • •

The bones of my left foot
are too heavy on the bones

of my right. They
lie still for a little while,

sleeping, but soon they
bruise each other like

angry twins. Then
the bones of my right foot

command the bones of my left
to climb down.

Two Poems

Peripheral

Maybe it's a bat's wings
at the corner of your eye, right
where the eyeball swivels
into its pocket. But when
the brown of your eye turns
where you thought the white saw,
there's only air and gold light,
reality—as your mother defined it—
milk/no milk. Not for years
did you learn the word "longing,"
and only then did you see the bat—
just the fringe of its wings
beating, its back in a heavy
black cloak.

Bird

The secret is
not to be afraid, to
pour the salt, letting your wrist
be free—there is almost
never too much; it sits on top of the skin like a
little crystal casket. Under it the bird might
imagine another life, one in which it is grateful
for pleasing, can smell
itself cooking—the taste
of carrots, onions, potatoes stewed
in its own juice—and forget
the dreams of blood
coursing out of its throat like a river.

1:30 A.M.

She can't sleep.
Is she unhappy? Depressed?
Does she need a pill? Is it
her nature? Bottom line: to endure
& write. No pills, no end to
therapy
in sight.
Is there a woman in there
who can't speak?

It's herself
she can't stand.
She's her own worst enemy.
That's obvious.
Without herself she'd be much better off,
happy, successful,
able to take what she wanted, at least, ask,
good things would mean
something,
be a stepping stone.
"You start & build & tear it all down,"
a fortune-teller says.

She was miserable.
She left her husband.
She's still miserable.
Did she do the wrong thing?
Was her old misery just an illusion of
her new one, or vice versa?

Perhaps, eventually, if she had stuck it out,
she would have opened like a saint, gained true
cheerfulness, the kind that makes old people's
faces gleam, & be grateful for each little gift.
How can you tell whether, ever, to go forward
or remain? trapped?
bearing what won't abate?
What the Buddhists call
"The Wisdom of no escape,"
the Christians call
hell.

She meditates.

───────────────────

Her father owned a dog that used to hate
him. Whenever the dog would come up from the basement
he'd paw at the door
to go back down. He'd lie down by her father's recliner as if he were
trying to make him happy,
to show him, really, you aren't so bad.
Finally, he couldn't
take his own desire,
he'd start shifting, lifting
up, he'd whine like a dog
who has to pee.
He just wanted
to go back down there by himself
where it was cool & dark, the way someone
with a terrible headache will want to be
left alone, with a cool rag on her head.
Once, to get away, he jumped through the glass door in the kitchen.
and ran down the street bleeding.

Her father told the story as if he were bragging—
that something near him could be that afraid!

You'll never get better.
That thought keeps recurring.
You could get worse. A lot worse.
Some poet leapt off of a bridge.
You wouldn't do that.
You would check into the nearest hospital,
like a cheap hotel you could
always get a room in
if you discovered a huge roach in your bed.

Where's the victory?
Where's the meat?
A friend comes to the Village in 1970 & falls in love with a
hot dog.
Nathan's The All Beef Hot Dog
the sign says;
ten years later he comes back & notices
a change,
Nathan's The All Meat Hot Dog
and ten years later, another change,
Nathan's The All *American* Hot Dog
Memory fades, a few good
jokes remain.

Sex?
Catalogs may be necessary,
like those seeds that come from

faraway places that produce
the best flowers.
Dildos of all different colors!
The mailman lugs their weight
knowledgeably,
in spite of the euphemistic names.
For a logo,
there's a woman from a Picasso painting
with a satisfied grin & her hand on her belly.
Mona Lisa wore that look
a woman of a certain age would know.
A woman who knows how to please herself
is gentle,
is her own best lover.

———————————————

The man in the bookstore on Craig asks,
"Where have you been for the last eight years?"
You didn't think he knew your name.
"Buried," you answer.

Maybe you were like those locusts, red-eyed,
eating.
"Your shoulders used to be boxy,
   as if you were always trying.
   You're milder now," an old friend explains.

Dead Baby Speaks

i am taking in   taking in
like a lump of a dead baby
on the floor   mama kicks me
i don't feel anything

---

i am taking in   taking in
i am reading newspapers
i am seeing films
i am reading poetry
i am listening to psychiatrists, friends
someone knows the way
someone will be my mother
& tell me what to think

---

the dead baby wants to scream
the dead baby wants to drink warm milk
the dead baby wants to say to her mother
i can't always say the right thing
i'm not perfect
but i will not be a lump on the floor
the dead baby wants to kick her mother
the dead baby wants her mother to lie down & let herself be kicked
why not   she let father do it

---

how to separate
me from the dead baby
my mother from me
my mother from the dead baby

nothing is expected
nothing is expected
of you
you don't have to do this or say that
nothing is known
just be   be who you are
a little defiance   a little defense
say, if you want
i lifted up a little

there is that stunned moment when she shuts up & lets me speak
i have nothing to say

then i say
rotten mother who opened your legs
like iron gates & forced me into this prison
who lay among lilies & pressed me to your breasts, saying i will never be alone
        again
who wanted my soul for company, used my body in the place of your soul
who brought me up to the surface by straining off the rich dark broth
until what remained was as vaporous as the shadow of a shadow
whose breasts were bruised fruits
whose legs were swollen tree trunks, but when you were shaken, only one red apple
        fell
whose genitals hold me tethered, a string like a primate's tail, so that i am your
        monkey in the red hat, you are my organ grinder

if you say do not write about me
i will write more
there are many more mouths to feed

than yours
my life is juice pouring
out of me
let it find a channel

---

i could knuckle under & be good
i could pray for her & turn the other cheek
i could live in her house with her sickness like a stinking body in the stairwell
i could bake bread until my hands puff off
i could sweep the floor
i could suck misery out of my teeth like stringy meat
i could poison her with a plate of sorrow
i could leave the door open on her corpse so that no breath would warm her back to
        resurrection
i could throw myself at her feet
i could languish like a whore in colored rags
i could lie as still as a still life
i could be cut up & served on her table
i could go to my father & beg for her life
i could dance the seven veils while she escapes
i could give to the poor
i could close my legs like a hardened corpse
i could grow into a hag & compare myself to her pictures
i could eat her while she's sleeping
i could put her in the oven & burn her into a lace cookie
i could roar like a gored dragon
i could come crawling like a sexless husband
i could beg her to touch that scratch between my legs which should open in a flower

---

every time i question myself, i say
mother did not believe me

she thought i was making up my life to torture her
i take off the layers for her to see the teeth marks in my soul
she thinks i can be born fresh once my rotten desires are removed

the desire to touch
the desire to speak

i could clean house until it is empty
i could put everything in the right place
but what about the one mistake i always make

———————————————

i could love her
i could love her every time she is mistreated
i could love her every time someone forgets to pick up a plate from the table
i could love her weeping in church with a light on her face
i could love her stinking of Ben-Gay on the cot waiting for my father to come
i could love her roaming from room to room in the dark with a blanket on, trying to
        be quiet
i could love her eating at night, hungrily, slowly, going back for seconds
i could love her white breasts
i could love her belly of scars
i could love her insides which are half of a woman's
i could love her with the dead baby in her
i could love her though the dead baby could be me
i could love her even if she wants some part of me dead
some part that invades her with sorrow she never understands

———————————————

for the mystery of her childhood
for being too white & too black
for being robbed of a father
for wearing the cast-off clothes of the rich

for eating figs & cream on silver that wasn't hers
for putting the comb & brush neatly in place because they were the only things she
       owned
for learning to make up lies & make everything pretty
(she never believed her own body)
i could love her ocean black hair
i could love it in a braid like a long black chain
i could love her kneeling over the tub cleaning the scum out with a rag
i could love her trying to hit the flying roach with a shoe
i could love her standing in the doorway, thinking she's made the wrong choice

as frail as i
as strange to herself as i
as beautiful as i
as ugly as i

i could do all these things & never be happy

_____

worse was done to me she said *& i never told*
i always told
in the body out the mouth
everything from insults to penises
needed words to make it real
be still   you make me suffer
i thought it was i who would die
i thought silence was a blessing
& i was its saint
i was prepared for
a higher calling

_____

we are fighting for my silver soul
like Jacob & the angel
you are the angel
i am the young boy fighting for my life
i am the angel
you are the young boy fighting for your life
we mirror each other
like a beautiful face in the river
half of us is drowned
half of us is light
i reach into your soul & pull out the bone of my life

---

my mother is on my mouth
like a frog
be good be good
she points her finger, that old spinster teacher
she points her stick at my tongue
she knocks some sense into it across its red knuckle
half of my tongue hangs like a limp dick
a flag of my mother's country
half rises like a bridge
words might leap across that great divide, a daredevil driver
but i am the driver
& my mother is peeping out of the back like a baby
her eyes big & black with fear

---

my mother is on my mouth
like a gold frog
she is sparkling & quick as sin
with terrible humped breasts

that nothing can suck at
the black spots on her are universes you could walk on
if she were flat & sound as a board
i take her on my tongue like a lozenge
& roll her around
then i bite down

The Origins of the Artist: Natalie Cole

My father
was black, black

as suede,
black as the ace

of spades, black
as the grave. Black

humbled him
and made him

proud. At first
there was a space

between us,
a mirror flashed

back at me. Then
his blackness

entered
me like God.

From a Letter: About Snow

for Chana Bloch

I am at a retreat house,
and the nun who runs the house told me to look at my face in the mirror.
I did, but the only thing I keep seeing is the face of Snow, the huge Pyrenees
     sheep dog.
He's so frightened, they can't let him off his leash!
His human eyes, long-suffering, like a saint who's forgotten how to smile.
I hear the breed is naturally shy, and this one was abused by his previous owner.
No wonder he backs away!
But to see a creature so large—120 pounds—so timid.
Once, they say, scared by a deer, he broke his leash and ran.
A mile away a woman stopped with her pickup and he jumped right in!
Who knows why the frightened make decisions!
Today I jogged with him, his thick rangy self leading the way.
Now we're sitting in the shade by the community house while I write this letter.

Not Forgotten

I love the way the black ants use their dead.
They carry them off like warriors on their steel
backs. They spend hours struggling, lifting,
dragging (it is not grisly as it would be for us,
to carry them back to be eaten),
so that every part will be of service. I think of
my husband at his father's grave—
the grass had closed
over the headstone, and the name had disappeared. He took out
his pocket knife and cut the grass away, he swept it
with his handkerchief to make it clear. "Is this the way
we'll be forgotten?" And he bent down over the grave and wept.

Grace Paley Reading

Finally, the audience gets
restless, & they send me
to hunt for Grace. I find her
backing out of the bathroom, bending
over, wiping up her footprints
as she goes with a little
sheet of toilet paper, explaining,
"In some places, after the lady mops,
the bosses come to check on her.
I don't want it to look
like she didn't do her job!"

Clitoris

This time with your mouth on my clitoris, I will not think
he does not like the taste of me. I lift the purplish hood back
from the pale white berry. It stands alone on its thousand branches.
I lift the skin like the layers of taffeta of a lady's skirt.
How shy the clitoris is, like a young girl
who must be coaxed by tenderness.

The Undertaker's Daughter

• • •

The dreadful war nature wages
to prevent the Poet from existing.
GEORGE SEFERIS, *Days of 1945–1951*

Preface to *The Undertaker's Daughter*

Voyage through death,
voyage whose chartings are unlove.
ROBERT HAYDEN

An apology to the reader

Let me first say that I regret sending this document out into the world.
And I regret that it has fallen into your hands and that, it having fallen
into your hands, I am asking you to read it. However, after having
put it away for years, then worked on it through thousands of drafts,
I decided that it should be—even must be—given space.

I do this not as a performance of brutality to which I need your witness.
I do it because it must exist as a reflection of its contrary. In my body
the memories were lodged. This writing is a dim bulb on a black cord
in the examiners' room.

I prefer that you do not attempt to read it. I cannot help but feel
responsible for your discomfort, so as you read you may feel me slightly
tugging it from your fingers. The revelations are relentless, without
a whisper of hope. (Without hope, what gives the poet permission?)
I send this document of torture out because it happened to me and
happened continuously inside me for seventy years.

Completing a work of art necessitates a struggle to create balance
and symmetry. I have been hampered by an idea of perfection. I have
struggled to please one who mirrors back my unworthiness. But poetry
comes from inside; it is visceral; it recreates the most primal sense of
entitlement to breath and music, to life itself.

I have fixed together an internal form, like a tailor's bodice. I wear it as
a self, stiff but useful, pieced together from scraps. Through it, in this
new incarnation, I am as vulnerable as a self without mirror.

PART I
The Undertaker's Daughter

I am not afraid to be memoir

*Before the amphetamine of accomplishment; when there was only a
physical body and a mind circulating through it like blood, with hardly
a hovering angel, chunky, spirited, too big for her britches, on the
two-wheeler before the grown-ups rose, driving the neighbors crazy on
Sunday morning when the neighborhood should be quiet, first tendency
to test, legs and eyes, standing up on the seat with one leg out behind her,
one or two hands on the handlebars, like a circus lady riding bareback,
back to loneliness, back back before angels separated and became the
mad god.*

*I want to go back there, without a platform except that rising of the
body itself, that challenge up to being, I want to go back to where the
first and last wisdom forms, the secret self locked in the tentative field
of protoplasm, whatever was cooled and cooked on the rock, whatever
mitochondria god stuck his thumb in, back back, I am not afraid to be
memoir.*

Beds

Trauma is not what happens to us, but what we hold inside us in the absence of an empathetic witness.

PETER LEVINE, *The Unspoken Voice*

I.

The first was a bassinet. I don't remember what it was made of; I think it was one of those big white wicker baskets with wheels. When I couldn't sleep at night, my father would drag it into the kitchen. It was winter. He'd light the gas oven. I remember the room's stuffiness, the acrid bite of cold and fumes.

My father didn't like crying. He said I was doing it to get attention. He didn't like my mother teaching me that I could cry and get attention. Nothing was wrong with me, and, even if I was hungry, it wasn't time to eat. Sometimes, I screamed for hours, and my father—I do remember this—would push his chair up to the lip of the bassinet and smoke, as if he were keeping me company.

After a few nights, he had broken me. I stopped crying. But, when he put the bottle to my lips, I was too exhausted to drink.

II.

My second was a crib in the corner of my parents' room. We moved to the attic when I was eighteen months old, so it must have been before that. I still didn't sleep at night. I'd see a huge gray monster outside the window, swaying toward me and side to side. I was afraid that, any moment, it would swoop in and get me. But I couldn't wake my parents. What if it wasn't real but only the huge blue spruce outside the window? If I woke them for nothing my father would be angry. I was more afraid of my father than I was of the monster. If I just kept watching, it couldn't get me.

III.

My aunt brought home a present for me every day when she came from
work. I'd wait by the kitchen door as soon as I could walk. Sometimes,
she'd fish down in her pocketbook, and the only thing she could find
was a Tums, which she called candy. But mostly she'd bring colored
paper and pencils from the printing press where she worked.

When I was two or three, I began to draw things and to write my
name. I wrote it backward for a long time: "I-O-T." I drew houses, cars,
money, and animals. I actually believed everything I drew was real; the
house was a real house, as real as the one we lived in. I held it in my
hand. It belonged to me, like a chair or an apple. From then on, I did
not understand my mother's sadness or my father's rage. If we could
have whatever we wanted just by drawing it, there was nothing to miss
or to long for. I tried to show them what I meant, but they shrugged it
off, not seeing or believing.

(*This sideways escape—the battle between my father's worst thought
of me and this proof, this stream of something, questioned and found
lacking, which must remain nearly invisible—pressed into what leaks out as
involuntarily as urine, a message which must be passed over the coals, raked,
purified into a thin strand of unambiguous essence of the deep core.*)

IV.

When I was seven, we moved to the Forest Lodge. We lived in D12
on the fourth floor. My mother and father slept in the living room on
a bed that came down out of the wall. I slept on a rollaway cot kept in
the same closet and pulled out at night. I helped my mother roll it into
a corner of the kitchen, push the kitchen table back and open the cot,
its sheets and blankets still tight. (Whatever I had, I kept nice. I had to.
My bed was my bed, but it was in my mother's space. If she needed the
space, my bed would go.)

Someone had given me an easel-shaped blackboard with a sheet of clear plastic that you could pull down and paint on. In the morning, my mother would set it up in a small area between the dining room and the kitchen. She didn't mind if the colors spilled, if a few drops fell on the newsprint she had put down. After she scrubbed every Saturday, she liked to put newspaper over the linoleum to keep it clean of our footprints. Wednesday, halfway through the week, she'd take the torn, dirty papers up, and, underneath, the floor was like new.

V.

Most times I liked my food. I didn't mind eating until my daddy started making me clean my plate and either struck me off my chair if I didn't or lifted me up by my hair and held me midair if I was slow. He wanted me to eat faster; he didn't have all day.

He'd hold me off the floor until I pleaded. I'd sputter in fear and humiliation—I don't remember pain—but I had to button up before he put me down to do exactly what he had told me to do, fast.

Slowness was a sign of insubordination. If I missed a pea or a crumb, I was trying to outwit him. I must have thought he was stupid. And if I pleaded that I hadn't seen the pea, he'd know I was lying. "Your story is so touching till it sounds like a lie."

I swallowed it down; I wiped that look off my face. But still he would notice my bottom lip beginning to quiver. This was a personal insult, as if I had taken a knife and put it to his face. If my brow wrinkled in a question—"Do you love me, daddy? How could you hurt me like this?"—this implied I was pursuing my own version of the truth, as if I were his victim.

It was a war of wills, as he so clearly saw, and these were my attempts to subvert him, to make my will reign.

He was the ruler of my body. I had to learn that. He had to be deep in me, deeper than instinct, like the commander of a submarine during times of war.

VI.

Thinking was the thing about me that most offended or hurt him, the thing he most wanted to kill. Just in case my mind might be heading in that direction, here was a stop sign, a warning: "Who do you think you are?" But the words weren't enough. They'd bubble out of him like some brew exploding from an escape hatch, a vortex that pulled in his whole body, his huge hands, which grabbed me up by my hair.

Where could I go? I was trapped in what my father thought I was thinking. I couldn't think. My thinking disappeared in case it was the wrong thought.

It was not the world that I needed to take in, but my father's words. I had to see exactly what my father saw in me—and stay out of its way.

VII.

In the morning, I'd fold up my bed and put it away. On those days and nights when my father didn't come home, we didn't need the space in the kitchen for breakfast or dinner, so we didn't put my bed away. I'd make it without a wrinkle, the pillow placed carefully on top, and it would stay in the little space under the window.

Maybe the black phone had rung saying he'd be late. Or maybe she had put him out.

I didn't know how they slept in the same bed because they never touched. Once, I saw them kiss. Maybe it was her birthday or Mother's Day. They blushed when they saw I saw them.

VIII.

I am trying to get as close as possible to the place in me where the change occurred: I had to take that voice in, become my father, the judge referred to before any dangerous self-assertion, any thought or feeling. I happened in reverse: my body took in the pummeling actions, which went down into my core. I ask myself first, before any love or joy or passion, anything that might grow from me: "Who do you think you are?" I suppress the possibilities.

IX.

My mother used the small inheritance she received from her mother to put my father through embalming school. He moved to Chicago for the few months of training at Worsham, the college for black undertakers. She hoped to raise us up—her mother had been a cook—to become an undertaker's wife, one of the highest positions of black society. But when he came back from the school, my father wouldn't take the mean $5 a week his stepfather offered him to apprentice. He wouldn't swallow his pride. He also wouldn't take jobs offered by his stepfather's competitors. That, too, was a matter of pride, not to sell out the family name.

My father never did practice undertaking for a living. Though, sometimes, when I was young, friends would ask him to embalm someone they loved and my father would acquiesce. He would enter the embalming room at Webster's Funeral Home, put on the robe, take up the tools, and his stepfather would step back. His reputation grew in this way. People who saw the bodies he had worked on—especially the body of the beautiful and wealthy Elsie Roxborough, who died by her own hand and was buried in a head-to-foot glass casket like Sleeping Beauty—marveled at his art and agreed he had the best touch of anyone.

People praised him for conducting the most elegant service; for knowing exactly what to say to comfort the bereaved, for holding their arms and escorting them to the first funeral car, for convincing those who needed to cry that it was all right; yet knowing too how to quiet them so there were no embarrassing "shows."

My father knew the workings of the heart; that's why so many people—my grandmother; his stepfather; and even his best friend Rad, whose heart he had crushed—loved him even after he let them down completely and many times, even after he abandoned them or did the meanest things. My father was with each of them, holding their hands, when they died. My handsome, charming father, the ultimate lover, the ultimate knower of the heart.

X.

My father knew all about the body. He had learned in embalming school. For a while after his mother died, he stopped smoking and drinking and came home at night. He'd get out the huge leather-bound dictionary (Webster's—the same as our last name!) that my grandmother had given him when he graduated. He would open it to a picture of the bones in the middle of the book, which had three see-through overlays: on the first, the blue muscles; on the second, the red blood vessels; and, finally, on the third, the white nerves.

He loved the body, loved knowing how things worked. He taught me the longest name of a muscle, the sternocleidomastoid, a cradle or hammock that was strung between the sternum and mastoid. He'd amaze me with long, multisyllabic words; then he'd test me on the spelling.

My father always explained. He always showed me the little smear on the plate that I had set to drain before he'd make me do all the dishes over again. He'd explain how he had studied hard so he knew where to hit me and not leave a single mark. He'd brag about it. He wanted me to appreciate the quality of his work. Like any good teacher, he wanted to pass it down.

XI.

During the summer when my mother and aunt were cleaning and wanted me out of the house, I would go out to the side of the house with a flyswatter and command the flies not to land on my wall. There were hundreds of flies, and though I told them not to, they continued to land. I don't think I said it out loud. I think I said it—screamed it, really—in my mind. Sometimes, I believed that the things in the world heard your thoughts, the way God heard your prayers. When I was very young, not even out of my crib, I'd ask the shades to blow a certain way to prove they had heard me.

The flies were disobeying me. Whenever one landed, I would go after it with the flyswatter. I was furious that they would do what I had commanded them not to. I knew they understood, or would understand finally. I killed tens, hundreds—didn't they see?—but they wouldn't stop.

I knew I was murderous, and yet, was it murder to kill flies? My aunt and mother never stopped me.

XII.

Before my grandmother died when I was ten, she had three dogs. Each had a short life. Patsy was the "good" dog who died of a chicken bone in her stomach, and Smokey was the "bad" dog who growled at people and would jump over the second-story banister on the porch and walk around on the outside of the rail. When my grandmother and grandfather were downstairs in the undertaking parlor, they would leave me alone with Smokey. I was about seven and I had learned the voice the nuns used to say cruel things to the children who were slow. Sometimes, the nuns hit those children over the knuckles with a ruler, but mostly they just humiliated them, made them sit in the back and never called on them to do errands. I tried to teach Smokey to stay behind the gate to the pantry. I would open the gate and tell him to stay, and when he went out in the kitchen, I'd hit him with his leash. I believe I hit him hard, maybe as hard as my father hit me. I wanted to feel that power.

I did this two, three, or four times and, though it seems impossible that my grandparents didn't know, no one stopped me. One time I came over, and my grandmother said Smokey had run away, jumped over the second-story banister to the street and didn't die. He was never

seen again. Was he that desperate to get away? I felt sad and responsible.
I felt glad.

XIII.

I was nine when we moved to a bigger apartment on the first floor.
Now, my father had only one flight to carry me up by my hair. He
didn't mind going public—the stairs were right in the lobby—but
he refused to allow me to scream in terror when he grabbed me. Not
because he was afraid people would see. My screaming made him
furious because I knew he was only going to carry me up the stairs and
scream at me, only beat me on the thighs and calves (where it wouldn't
show), and only until I made every look of pain, confusion, and fury
disappear. He knew I knew that. So what was all that broadcasting, as if
something really bad was going to happen, as if he was going to kill me?

XIV.

Life is something you have to get used to: what is normal in a house, the
bottom line, what is taken for granted. I always had good food. Our
house was clean. My mother was tired and sad most of the time. My
mother spent most of her day cleaning.

We had a kitchen with a little dining space, a living room, a
bedroom, a bathroom and two halls, one that led to the bathroom and
the bedroom, and one that led to the front door. There was a linen
closet in the hall between the bedroom and the bathroom. My books
and toys all went into a drawer that I had to straighten every Saturday.
There was a closet in the bedroom for my mother's clothes, a closet in
the front hall for my father's, and a closet off the living room that held
my mother's bed.

It was a huge metal apparatus that somehow swept out on a hinge.
I can't imagine how my mother and I, as small as we were, brought it
out and put it back every night and every morning, for my father was

hardly ever there. We just grabbed on, exerted a little force, and pulled it straight toward us. It seemed to glide by itself, swinging outward around the corner; then it would stand up, rocking, balancing, until we pulled it down.

XV.

My father and I shared the small bedroom, and my mother slept on the pullout in the living room so that she wouldn't wake us when she got dressed in the morning to go to her new job. We slept in twin beds she had bought us, pushed up close together.

I had special things given to me, special things she paid for: the expensive toys I got for Christmas that took a whole year to pay for and the clothes I wore from Himelhoch's while my mother wore an old plaid coat for eleven years. Now I was a big girl moving from a little cot in the kitchen to my own bed in a bedroom. My father and I always got the best.

XVI.

My mother shopped after work every Thursday, so my father would come home and fix dinner for me. He'd stop at Fadell's Market and get a big steak with a bone in it. He'd bring it home and unwrap the brown paper, slowly, savoring one corner at a time, like someone doing a striptease or opening a trove of stolen diamonds. He'd brag about how much money he had spent. He'd broil it right up next to the flame, spattering grease, fire, and smoke, only a couple of minutes on each side, cooked still bloody, nearly raw, the way we liked it, he said—different from my mother. He'd say he liked it just knocked over the head with a hammer and dragged over a hot skillet. His eyebrows would go wild, and he'd rub his hands together like a fly.

XVII.

Once, my father took me to the movies. We walked downtown to the Fox Theater on one unusually warm Thursday evening during my Christmas vacation to see Bing Crosby in *The Bells of St. Mary*. My father frequently promised things he didn't deliver, like the time he promised to come home and pray the family rosary every night for a week when I carried the huge statue of the Virgin home in a box as big as a violin case. He never came home once. When I turned the Virgin back in at school, I had to lie to the nun. After that, I rarely asked for anthing. But going to the movies was his idea.

I was never happier than when I was with my father and he was in a good mood. He liked to tease me and make me laugh. He was so handsome that I felt proud when people noticed us. I thought they were thinking that my father really enjoyed me, that I was a very special girl. I acted like a special girl, happy and pretty, until I almost believed it. I had dressed up, and we stopped for a Coney Island and caramel corn, which were his favorites.

XVIII.

By this time, my father didn't come home most nights. Sometimes, he and my mother wouldn't speak to each other for months. Sometimes, they wouldn't speak even to me when we were in the house together, as if we had to be quiet, like in church, and respect their hatred for each other.

My father thought I hated him like my mother did or else he didn't think I was worth talking to, for he'd often go months without speaking even when we were in the house alone.

I tried to make him change. I'd make up special names like "D-dats." "Hi D-dats," I'd meet him at the door when he came home at night. I knew he liked to feel young and hip. I'd make my voice happy, as if I weren't afraid he'd find a shoe or book out of place and beat me. I actually was happy when I was with him—I had to be! He could see inside me. He could tell my moods. My unhappiness blamed him.

Maybe all that silence and beating was because he thought nobody loved him, not my mother and not his mother. He told me how his mother had knocked him down when he was a grown man. He told me how my mother always picked up his ashtrays to wash them as soon as he put his cigarette out. I tried to make him feel loved. Sometimes, we played "Step on a crack you break your mother's back" when we were coming home from his mother's house, as if the two of us were in cahoots.

XIX.

Once, when I was ten or eleven, he came home for lunch, and I asked him if I could dance for him. I had seen Rita Hayworth dance the Dance of the Seven Veils. I had stayed home sick and practiced. I liked to dance on the bed so I could see myself in my mother's dressing table mirror.

I wore old see-through curtains and my mother's jewelry on my head like a crown. I must have had something underneath for I knew some things mustn't show. I thought, maybe, if he saw I was almost a woman and could do what beautiful women do, he might find a reason to love me.

At the end, I spun around and around until most of the drapes, towels, and my mother's nightgown fell to the floor. I don't remember what remained to cover me.

XX.

Sometimes, on the nights he came home, I'd sneak up on him while he was reading the newspaper and pull off his slipper.

He'd put the paper down very deliberately, put on his "mean" play-face and say, "Oh, you want to play, huh?" And he'd grab me up like an ogre. He'd hold me down and jab his fingers into my ribs.

"No," I'd scream, "I'm sorry," and I'd plead that I would pee if he didn't let me up.

Finally, he'd relent. "You're not going to do it again?" And he'd tickle me more.

"Never, never," I'd scream.

"Are you sure?"

As soon as he picked up the paper again and seemed to turn his attention away, I'd go back.

My father could make me laugh. He knew just where to hit the funny bone. Always, my father was the only one who could make me swallow pills or sit still while he administered burning iodine. When I fell or took the wrong step over a picket fence, I'd come to him, crying. "I'm going to have a big scar and nobody will love me." And he'd tease, "Oh, my poor little baby, all the boys are going to call her 'old scar leg,' and she's going to be alone for the rest of her life"; but he'd do what had to be done, hold the leg in place, put the iodine on the raw spot, right where it was needed, direct and quick, without flinching, never afraid to cause the necessary pain.

XXI.

On Saturday mornings, my mother and I would have toast and coffee in her bed. She let me lie there while she planned our day. She'd get up barefoot and put the coffee on and make me sugar toast. I loved those Saturday mornings near her: her big bed, her cold cream smell.

I had always thought my mother was frightened of my father. She never seemed to fight straight. She got him by going the back route, like the look on her face when she got in the orange and yellow truck that he bought when he started the egg business. She sat on the orange crate—he called it the passenger seat—and never laughed, never joined in on the fun as he took us around Belle Isle. He had been so happy when he jingled the keys, but you could tell she thought that old truck was nothing to be proud of, as if even a joke about such a poor thing was in bad taste.

Then one Saturday morning, I spotted a big roach, a water-bug, on the living room floor. I jumped up on the bed and started screaming; she came from the kitchen, grabbed her house shoe and got down on all fours. The thing charged her from under the chair like a warrior. I was screaming like crazy. I realized she was my last protection. And she started punching at the thing, punching the floor, anywhere she could punch. She didn't stop until it was flattened.

I had never seen my mother brave. I had never seen that she would fight to the death. It was a part of her she never showed. I had thought she didn't stop my father from beating me because she was afraid. I was confused by her braveness.

XXII.

My mother was sad. She didn't feel appreciated. I didn't do enough to help. She hurt inside. Her body suffered. Her feet swelled black with poison. She had a dead baby. She had womb problems. They had to take the knotted thing out. The doctor rubbed her stomach for hours until she went to the bathroom. She got TB. She got a goiter. She shouldn't clean so hard; she should rest, at least late in the afternoon. But she wouldn't. She had to keep doing what hurt her.

My mother and father were at war; whoever loved the other first would lose.

XXIII.

Nobody thought the little marks were worth looking at. I cried and showed how they went up my arm all the way to my elbow, ran all over my ankles and the tops of my feet, even up my thighs. I could see them, but when anyone else looked, the marks disappeared.

Maybe they didn't itch. Maybe they weren't serious. Maybe I was causing trouble. (I had an active imagination, my mother and father said.) I couldn't sleep because something was happening in my bed—a misery—and everybody acted as if it wasn't. It didn't hurt after a while. I could take my mind off it and put it somewhere else.

I think the only reason my mother finally believed me was because I kept showing her that Monday mornings, after I had spent the weekend with my aunt, I didn't have the marks, but Tuesdays, after I had slept in my own bed, I had the marks again.

In an instant of recognition, she raced into the bedroom, flipped my covers off the bed and saw the little bits of blood. She turned over the mattress, and there, in the corners, were the nests of a thousand bedbugs, lethargic or crawling. She looked close. They had gotten so far inside that the room had to be sealed with tape, a bomb put in.

He had been sleeping with another woman. He had brought her dirt into his own home (though he said the bugs came in egg crates).

Bedbugs were what poor women had, women who couldn't do better, women who didn't matter. Some other woman's bedbugs were making my mother the same as that woman.

He had brought in everything she hated, everything she couldn't control: the helplessness of slavery, bad births, poverty, illness, death. Everything she had risked her life to clean out of our apartment.

My mother had reason for outrage.

I only had reason to itch.

XXIV.

The living room was off limits. There was too much that might get messed up or broken. I guess he chose rooms to beat me in honor of the sacrifices my mother had made to make our home beautiful.

In the bedroom, where could I go when I fell? I wouldn't fall on the wooden footboards. There was an aisle between my mother's closet and my father's bed. That was too narrow. On the left side of the doorway was my mother's dressing table, where I'd sit and put on necklaces, earrings, and nail polish and look in the mirror. There wasn't room for me to flail around, so my father had to be very specific about the direction in which his blows would aim me.

If my cousin was visiting, he would inform her, his voice sincere but matter-of-fact—"I'm going to have to take Toi to the bathroom." He preferred the bathroom when she was visiting, except when my mother was in on it, and then we needed a bigger space. If, for example, my mother had told him I talked back, he'd say, "We're going to have to speak to Toi in the kitchen." He'd pull me by my arm and close the kitchen door, which had glass panes so that my cousin could see.

But she said she averted her eyes, knowing it would humiliate me. She remembers him sliding off his belt; she remembers me pleading each time the belt hit; she remembers him telling me, as he was beating me, in rhythm, why he was doing it and what I shouldn't do the next time. I would come out, trying not to show how I had been afraid for my life, how I had pleaded without pride. I thought those things would have made her hate me.

• • •

I remember the hitting, but not the feeling of the hits; I remember falling and trying to cover my legs with my hands.

I remember the time I came home with a migraine and begged him not to beat me. "Please, please, daddy, it hurts so bad." I could hardly speak. I had to walk level, my head a huge cup of water that might spill on the floor.

Why couldn't he see my pain? My head seemed to be splitting open, my eyes bleeding. I didn't know what might happen if I tipped my head even slightly. He saw me walking like that, as if someone had placed delicate glass statues on my arms and shoulders. I begged him, *not now*. I knew I had it coming. I had gone out with the Childs, and he had left a note telling me not to go out.

• • •

The Childs lived on the fourth floor. Sometimes, they brought down the best rice with butter and just the right amount of salt and pepper. They had no children. They had a little bubble-shaped car. We all seemed glad to roll the windows down and go out to their niece's. She turned her bike over to me. It was so much fun pumping it up and down the hill, letting my hair fly. I forgot my father, as I had forgotten the bug bites, as I forgot what it felt like to be beaten. I just thought, *I'm pumping harder so I will go faster and let the air hit my face and arms, and then I'll stop pumping at the top and fall down and down, my feet up off the pedals.* And I didn't feel fat: My body lost weight—it just went with everything going in that direction, and the wind flew against me in the other direction. Though it blew in my face and began to sting, I couldn't stop pumping, couldn't stop trying, one more time, to bring myself to that moment of pleasure and accomplishment right before I'd let go.

I had never felt such power, earning it by my own work and skill. I could ride it. I was the girl in charge; I had the power to bring myself there.

XXV.

Shortly after I was married, we had a dog that kept shitting on the floor. Once, I took a coat hanger and was going to hit her with it, but she drew back her lips and snarled at me in self-defense and fury. I had no idea that she would defend herself. I was shocked. I thought she was going to attack me, and I put the hanger down. I respected her in a different way after that.

She lived for sixteen years and was a great mothering presence in our household. It seemed every dog and cat that came in the house had to lie beside her, with some part of its body—a paw, the hind— touching hers. Once, I heard a strange noise during the night and went to investigate. A kitten my son had found on the railroad tracks was nursing from her, and she was sleeping, as if she just expected to be a mother. When I would come home, after I had been away for a while, she'd jump up on the bed and curl her butt into my belly, and I'd put my arms around her and hold her like a lover. When she died, I missed her so much I realized that she had been my mother, too. She taught me it was beautiful to defend yourself—and that you could be unafraid of touch.

• • •

I remember how, occasionally, my father's dogs would pull back and snarl at him when he was viciously beating them. His anger would increase immeasurably. They had truly given him a reason to kill them. "You think you can get away with that in my house?" he'd ask, the same as he'd ask me.

Once, to get away from him, one of his dogs leapt through the glass storm door in the kitchen and ran down 14th Street bleeding to death.

XXVI.

You would think that the one treated so cruelly would "kill" the abuser, throw him out of the brain forever. What a horrific irony that the abuser is the one most taken in, most remembered; the imprint of those who were loving and kind is secondary, like a passing cloud. Sometimes, I thought that's why my father beat me. Because he was afraid he would be forgotten. And he achieved what he wanted.

In the deepest place of judgment, not critical thinking, not on that high plain, but judgment of first waking, judgment of the sort that decides what inner face to turn toward the morning—in that first choosing moment of what to say to myself, the place from which first language blossoms—I choose, must choose, my father's words.

The twisted snarl of his unbelief turned everything good into something undeserved, so that nothing convinces enough—no man or woman or child, no play or work or art. There is no inner loyalty, no way of belonging. I cannot trust what I feel and connect to; I cannot love or hold anything in my hand, any fragile thing—a living blue egg, my own baby—in the same way that I never convinced my father I was his. And I must rest on it, as on bedrock.

XXVII.

The time I had the migraine, after my father had beaten me, he made me bathe. He drew the bath, felt the water with his fingers and made sure it wouldn't burn. He told me to go in there and take off my clothes.

The water, when I put my toe in, was like walking in fire. I stood there, holding myself.

And then—instead of letting my father kill me or bashing my own head against the tile to end all knowing—I crouched down, letting the lukewarm water touch me.

Oh, water, how can you hurt me this bad? What did I do to you? I was whimpering. I don't know if I still had hope he would hear me, or if I just couldn't stop the sound from leaking out of my body.

But my father came and lifted me out of the water in his arms, took me naked, laid me on my bed and covered me lightly with a sheet. Then he went away and left me in the dark as if to cool down, and he brought cut lemon slices for my eyes and a cool towel or pads of alcohol to put on my forehead. He bathed me in tenderness, as if he really knew I was suffering and he wanted me to feel better.

I wondered if he finally believed. If he realized from within himself that I had been telling the truth, that I wasn't evil. Maybe he had some idea of how much he had hurt me. I knew that, sometimes, men beat their women and then make up. I didn't know which daddy was real.

Afterword:

I hear in myself a slight opposition, a wounded presence saying, I am me, I know who I am. But I am left with only a narrow hole, a thin tube that the words must squeak through. Where words might have gushed out as from a struck well, now, instead, I watch it—watch every thought. It wasn't my father's thought that I took in; it was his language. It is the language in me that must change.

The undertaker's daughter

Terrified at a reading to read
poems about my fears & shames,

a voice in me said: *Just
open your mouth*. Now

I read about Anubis, the God of Egypt

who ushered the dead
to the underworld, who performed the ritual of

the opening of the mouth

so they could
see, hear & eat.

Had it been my father speaking,

giving me back that
depth of taste & color,

fineness of sound
that his rages stifled,

twisted & singed shut? I had thought

it was a woman's voice—
though I had hoped

all my life that my father would feed me
the milk my mother could not

make from her body.
Once, when I opened the door & saw

him shaving, naked, the sole of his foot
resting on the toilet, I thought

those things hanging down were
udders. From then on I understood there was a

female part he hid—something
soft & unprotected

I shouldn't see.

Sunday afternoon at Claire Carlyle's

My mother & father, light-
skinned, but too new

to make the upper cut,

were, nevertheless, welcomed
into the marble foyer

under an icebox-sized chandelier
to mix martinis with double-edged

men and women trained to outwit
and out-white the whites. Almost all

were light & straight-featured
enough to pass—some did,

some didn't.
Claire's brother Bob

passed. If seen weekdays,
he wasn't

to be spoken to. Light and dark
did the same—an inward

move to protect those
fortunate enough to choose.

But why did my mother

(who looked as white
as Loretta Young—& as beautiful) see

Bob one weekday walking
toward her up Woodward

and cross
to the other side? Why,

when anyone would
only have seen

two white people?
It was something in my mother

not visible: in her

mind's eye
she was black & wore the robe

of it over her fine features. Perhaps,
she crossed in case

some inner misstep

might betray him
(the inner world

being vast & treacherous)—

as if they were slaves running
for their lives.

Dolls

To be born woman is to know—
Although they do not speak of it at school—
Women must labor to be beautiful.

W. B. YEATS

Teng ai, a love imbedded in preverbal knowledge,
accompanied by unspeakable pain, and shared
only through the empathy between the two bodies
(mother and daughter) alike.

WANG PING

I.

Take care of your little mother, my aunt told me
shortly before she died. My little five-foot-four-inch mother,
whose clothes I outgrew when I was ten, already
proud of my big bones—(Nothing could overpower
me if I was made of my father's bones). My mother was astounded—
I should put bricks on your head & she kept dressing me
in pinafores & ruffled socks. *Toi*, she called me,
as if I was supposed to stay small.

II.

Sometimes it seemed I couldn't have come out of
her, that something was wrong. When I stood behind her I felt
ungainly, like something that flopped about without
gravity. I was excessive, too much.
I thieved her clothes until it was impossible to make them
fit—hers was the only body I knew how to make beautiful.

III.

My grandmother bought me a doll I couldn't touch. She
had peaches & cream skin, breasts, a taffeta dress,
& porcelain green eyes. Her fingers were delicate & curved
like eyebrows. I broke my dolls, so we had to put her up
high to admire, like a storeowner sticks a manikin
on a black pole to show off what he's got.

IV.

My mother gave me dolls that peed, that you had to feed,
that you had to bathe in a little plastic Bathinette.
Everything smelled clean like rubber. You had to
learn to be a mother. Even the pee. One of the bottles
refilled itself when you turned it upright. It was o.k. for a
doll to pee. The more work you did the better mother you were.

V.

I was hard on my dolls. The ones that had stuffed bodies
came up missing arms. Monkey-bear had his insides ripped out.
Big Rabbit couldn't stand. His legs & feet were
bent forward so that, when we played school—with his
Little Buddha smile that,
no matter how much I swung him around in a circle & beat him
against the floor, just stayed there—he would topple off his
seat & have to be shaken again.

VI.

The dolls that cried *mamma* came up with a busted rattle in
their throat, their eyes clunked open so that they couldn't go to
sleep but stared perpetually up at the ceiling like middle-aged
insomniacs. One doll had a problem with her eyes, they were out
of kilter, so that they didn't open unless you whacked
her on the back. Then they were stuck open, so she seemed
dead. We had to work on her too hard to make her do the most
ordinary things—just to open her eyes! Her eyes clunked shut &,
way back in the pit of her skull, we could hear her thinking.

VII.

When I was born my mother sat up, hysterical, on the delivery
table. She said it was the drugs. She couldn't stop laughing.
Her toxemic body had been pumped out & I was a robin's egg
blue, a pale, delicate thing whose blood vessels you
could see from the outside. My "inner life" stared up at you
through translucent skin, the way you can see a face
floating up to a lake's surface.

I put my inner life right in her hands.

VIII.

No, that isn't the way my father saw it. He said
when he looked in the nursery he saw a baby so hairy
he thought it should be swinging from a chandelier.
Though he really loved me for my excesses—
for eating too much, for stealing French fries from his plate
(*That girl can really hold her liquor*, he'd brag
when I was twelve. *They call her old hollow leg*),
& even my hair—he'd lift me up by it
& carry me up four flights of stairs. He loved my hair.

IX.

My mother suffered, oh did she suffer, the way all
light-skinned women were supposed to suffer. She suffered that
& more. She proved that she didn't like it. She proved that of all
the un-black women, the ones babies didn't just come
popping out of—

                 & even of the ones that babies came roaring
through like a train, of even them—she was one of the most,
most suffering.

X.

During pregnancy, she wore the right shoes. She ate the
right foods. She read the book that the doctor gave her with
pictures of white women in plain suits. She tucked it in a place
sacred & hidden, in her sewing box. She pierced it with needles
& thread either punishing it or marking it
with a hundred little, colored banners.

She used to like sex, my
father once said, puzzled.

XI.

My mother with the peaches & cream skin, my mother with
the eyebrows of a blackbird's wing, my mother with eyelashes
that brushed halfway down her cheeks, my mother with the high,
creamy breasts, my mother in her slip & socks on her knees
scrubbing the kitchen floor, or weeping in the doorway,

my lovely, delicate, little mother.

Mistrust of the beloved

I must explain to you what I must explain to myself: that there, where love, desire and want spring from the most natural source, there, in that spot, in that moment, is the scalding fire; and, instead, springs to life the unwanted and beaten girl, her whole soul face and body shiny with burn scar, inflexible, taut and hard, immersed anew in the conflagration; for, as long as the route turns to that inward burning, it cannot take her out again into that place where her father proved he did not love.

The heart of one so riddled must keep to itself: We spoil what we want for the deeper motive, for it is deep in the brain where instinct lives, as another withdraws a hand from fire.

PART II
A Memory of the Future

I see my father after his death

I caught a plane at about eleven in the morning, and we were at the funeral home at about two. My father had been dead about ten hours. We had chosen the mortician who had been my grandfather's old competitor, whose son, unlike my father, had stayed in the family business. I wanted to see my father before he was "ready," but the mortician didn't want to take me back. He talked about germs, about me washing my hands after. I didn't know if he was afraid of my emotions—that I would burst into uncontrollable tears?—or if there was something back there he didn't want me to see. Maybe it was dirty, or maybe it just wasn't the rule—so often people can't break the rules.

It was clean, like an old-fashioned kitchen, with tile and stainless steel sinks and counters. There was a huge blue bottle in the corner with a siphon in it, a black-and-white tile floor. It looked efficient, not spiffed up like his French provincial waiting room. Then I came upon my father, swaddled in a layer of linen, zipped in plastic and bound with tape, his face the only part of him free.

The color was pure, as if he had been drained of age and illness. That look of dark acceptance, that fixed stare that penetrated without hope or understanding, had been left behind. There was a softness I had never seen, his forehead, unlined and smooth. He had been given a second beauty as a death-gift. The monster had flown out on its hard dark wings, and left behind, not a shell, but one tortured a lifetime and released.

• • •

Even when he had been in a coma—his legs inflexible, locked in fetal position, nurses turning his body every few hours like something basted over coals—I would take the covers back and look at him. It was under the pretext of seeing if he had bedsores, or if he was losing weight but, really, all I wanted to do was fix my eyes on his body—the same big toe as mine, the same twisted little toe, his thick knees, each like the end of a club. I stared as long as I wanted, unashamed, unafraid of my great love, unafraid he would leave me.

My father had lost his sexual beauty in his sixties. But in the days of his illness his body became lustrous, so full of energy and brightness that it seemed too hot to put my hands on.

After his surgery he had said, "You're not going to like what you see," but when he lifted his shirt I kissed the long, raw cut, which looked like two slabs of butchered ribs stapled together, and said, "You're still beautiful to me." I had always loved what he could never love in himself—even his wounds.

• • •

Though he had been dead for ten hours, someone told me it takes thirteen for the spirit to move on. So he had not gone yet; he was still partly there, seeping out in shallow expirations.

Certainly what one sees later, after the embalming, is an object made by the undertaker; it has nothing to do with the one dead. Though I hadn't been with him at death, I was there to see him before the embalming and, for the rest of my life, to know that look of calm that had come.

My cruel father had looked forward, seen heaven, and sent back this sign of peace.

• • •

That night I had a dream, but not a dream, for it was as real as this very moment, with all my feelings in it; and I didn't have any idea of how or why or when. Suddenly, as if I had just been born and didn't know anything before that, I didn't feel fear. Nothing else had happened, just that fear had been sucked out of me, and I didn't even remember it happening but just felt gratitude for an absence that made my life—I swear I am not making a metaphor—feel like heaven.

But as the night went on—it didn't feel like night, it felt like a trueness that made everything different and new—a worry began to encroach, a sliver of gray: "What if this fearlessness were taken away?" When I woke I felt such joy; I shook my husband and said, "I'm free, I'm different." And then I began to put my feet over the side of the bed, slowly, the ground coming up to meet me and, at that moment, when my feet touched the floor, something in me said, "Your father is dead," and I knew why I had felt so happy.

• • •

I had forgotten that moment until today, that happiness that had tarnished like silver, like an old old mirror in which I could no longer see my face. I don't know why I lost it, why that heaviness came back— for wasn't my father truly dead, didn't I no longer have to fear him?— but, in a few days, the wonder faded. My mind was not ready for such light. I had to dig my way out of darkness one weighty grain at a time, as if a memory of the future had visited.

My dad & sardines

my dad's going to give me a self
back.
i've made an altar called
The Altar for Healing the Father & Child,
& asked him what i could do
for him so he would
do nice for me. he said i should stop
saying bad things about him &, since
i've said just about everything bad
i can think of &, since . . . well,
no, i change my
mind, i can't promise
him that. but even healing is
negotiable, so, if he's in
heaven (or trying
to get in), it wouldn't hurt
to be in touch. the first thing i want is to be able to
enjoy the little things again—for example, to stop peeling
down the list of things i
have to do &
enjoy this poem, enjoy how, last night, scouring
the cupboards, i found a
can of sardines that
must be five
years old &, since i was home after a long
trip &, since it was 1 a.m. & i hadn't eaten
dinner &, since there was no other
protein in the house,
i cranked it open & remembered that
my dad loved

sardines—right before bed—with
onions & mustard. i can't get into
my dad's old heart, but i remember that look
on his face when he would
load mustard on a saltine cracker, lay a little
fish on top, & tip it with a juicy slice
of onion. then he'd look up from his soiled
fingers with one eyebrow
raised, a rakish
grin that said—*all*
for me!—as if he was
getting away
with murder.

The new pet

i don't want to worry about a fish   yet
here i am   when i am tired   going down & up two
flights of stairs to bring him clean spring water
to fill up his bowl   maybe he looked un-
happy because there was no current—the water was not
high enough to reach the motor—& he has grown used to
the big tank, the heater & water filter, for he began to flip
about & even leap up to my finger when he was hungry.
surely nothing will come to me for doing
good to a fish, & still i do it; though i often wish i had
a mean heart

The Telly Cycle

Joy is an act of resistance.

Why would a black woman
need a fish
to love? Why did she need a

flash of red, living, in the
corner of her eye? As if she could love nothing
up close, but had to step

away from it, come
back to drop a few seeds
& let it grab

on to her, as if it caught
her
on some hook that couldn't

hurt. Why did she need a fish,
a red
thorn or, among the thorns, that

flower? What does her love have to do
with five hundred years of
sorrow, then joy coming up like a

small breath, a
bubble? What does it have to do
with the graveyards of the

Atlantic in her mother's
heart?

For Telly the fish

Telly's favorite artist was Alice Neel.
When he first came to my house,
I propped up her bright yellow shade with open
window & a vase of flowers (postcard size)
behind his first fish bowl. I thought
it might give him something
to look at, like the center
of a house you keep coming
back to, a hearth, a root
for your eye. It was a
wondering in me that came up with that
thought, a kind of empathy
across my air & through his
water, maybe the first
word I cast out between us
in case he could
hear. Telly would stare at that painting
for hours, hanging there with his glassy
eyes wide
open. At night he wanted the
bottom, as if it were a warm
bed, he'd lie there
sort of dreaming, his eyes
gray & dim &
thoughtless. For months he came back
to her, the way a critic or lover
can build a whole
lifetime on the study of one
great work. I don't know why
he stopped, maybe it was when
he first noticed
me, the face above my hand

feeding for, sometimes, when I'd set the food
on top, he'd still watch me, eye
to eye, as if saying, food
isn't enough. Once, when I
bent, he jumped up out of the water & kissed
my lips. What is a fish's kiss like?
You'd think it would be
cold, slimy, but it was
quick, nippy, hard. Maybe it was just
what I expected. For all
our fears of
touch, it takes so long
to learn how to take in.

When he stopped coming
to the top, I guess I did all the wrong
things—the fish medicine
that smelled, measured
carefully for his ounce of weight—
for his gills worked
so hard & he lay still,
tipped over slightly
like a dead boat.
How do you stop the hurt
of having to breathe?

After, I took him to the middle of the
yellow bridge right near the
Andy Warhol museum—
I had put a paper towel
in a painted egg & laid him in it—
&, at the top,
I opened the casket & emptied him out
into the water.

Special ears

I liked him for his tailfin, which was long like a mermaid's & flowed like a
silver blue ruffle in the water,
larger than you'd expect a little fish's tail to be—

    generous, excessive, a bit astonishing, like a girl with too much hair!

Sometimes he would rise like a submarine, straight up, as if he would nip
my finger, *get out of my water*, his mouth would open like a little scoop of
blackness & let out one bubble, like a smoke ring of my father's, a message
from the underworld.

Another poem of a small grieving for my fish Telly

Perhaps I should forgive
Telly for dying in my care, *Just a
fish*, someone said, *Just*

get another. Lucille said
our power becomes
greater when we lose the flesh; so,

when I poured Telly out
of his painted casket (a little wooden
egg) out over the rail

into the all
becoming, was it a miracle
that he had lived, was it a miracle?

Once, when I prayed for a sign,

God opened the closed
vault of the sky, the sun popped out
& shone directly in my face, & hail, yes,

hail started falling (in July). I was
afraid to believe in love. *God,
don't waste your miracles on me.* &

the sun went back, like a face
retreating. Telly, you are bodi-
less, you are with my mother

& father. Say it wasn't my
fault you suffered, with your little
working gills, say you forgive me.

On the reasons I loved Telly the fish

Why would I say I was
"pathetic," when talking about my
life, why would I think of it as
"little"—my "little life," I said,
as if, looking back
at what kept me alive,
what I constructed to make my own
success, to regard that with
tenderness &
understanding—as something even
sweet &
marvelous—was
insane? Then maybe I began to
love Telly—
really nothing in the
grand scheme of things—the way that lady, when I told her that
I paid 100 dollars a month for someone to come in &
feed Telly when I was away, said—"but, Toi, how much
did Telly cost? $1.98? Well then why not just
flush him every time & get another?"
Whatever I said
to myself, whatever
I felt & did, that
kind of care was
silly,
nice, but, well, you know,
crazy, the way, when you grow up &
understand the great
things, a fish's life is
nothing, as if (& probably they can't
think or feel) there are much more

important things to
do to think about to
love & dedicate ourselves
to: there are
doctors, great
poets, there is
fine furniture, true love, children,
god, for
god's sake, there is everything to
remember, everything to be
worried & concerned about, as if I could
find it if I just kept
looking, something really
real out there always just outside of what I could
take in. & this was how I
stayed alive.

    My aunt took me to
her job from the time I was about
three. I'd go down to the
basement where she was
head of the mail department—first black woman to have such an
executive job in Detroit, even though it was
in the basement—I'd take up a little
desk in the corner & do whatever she said, open
the flaps of envelopes by the box—five hundred in a box, maybe
twenty boxes a day for ten cents a box &, with each box, I'd
compete with myself, each day,
to make more
money, & make enough
to buy my own
lunch, a corned beef sandwich at the
Broadway Market with

two halves of a new
dill & a fruit
punch, & sit there at the
marble counter enjoying
the warmth of meat,
the slop of mustard,
& the way the
rind of the bread was
just a little tough to
tear with your teeth.
I worked without
word,
away from the grownups, able to
make my own
way & feel
competent, as if I had a
place & something I could truly
do without making somebody
mad or un-
happy. &, just looking
back on myself, as if I were an eye
looking from a high
place, seeing that little
girl, counting the envelopes, boxes, making her
fingers go faster,
counting the boxes over & over because she'd
forget & had to make certain,
enjoying how many boxes were piling
up, how, yesterday, she did a box in ten minutes &
today she could do more than
two boxes in twenty (there was always a way to
try harder & give the day a good
reason.)

When I looked back
on that little five-year-old, six, seven, eight, nine,
it was as if I were a little
busy fish being watched by an
interested & even caring
owner, as if I had finally
bought myself.

Because I was good to Telly in his life,

because I taught him Alice Neel
& fed him frozen mealworms,
(until I found out he'd
lose his bright red tail color
for that pleasure),
because I never left him
alone when I traveled (never liking those
who said their betta did just fine
sitting on the edge of their office desk
over the long weekend—how would *you*
like it not to eat for three
days, I wanted to ask), for choosing
carefully among the pet
sitters, interviewing, looking for one who took a fish
seriously
& told betta stories about how smart they
are, coming up
to say hi in the morning, checking you
out with a certain calm or anxious
look in the eye, because
I believed
in one fish's
brain & life & skills &
emptied him out into the
thawing river saying
prayers for my
lover or husband or brother
of a year,
because of this I am certain
he sent me a
gift from the china blue

rivers of heaven, a lovely man, who
first kissed me on
that bridge,
sending a photo
after rain of "Kissing
Bridge underwater" scrawled with his loose
sprawling letters; because all things are
connected, a
circle,
bread on the water, as my mother said,
always comes home.

An apology to Telly the revolutionary

Love or respect, my father said,
you can't have both.

Last night, after the reading,

the audience
climbed to their feet

& cheered you—as if
you were a rock star!

Viva Telly!
Telly lives!

One woman explained,
you only let them *think* you were

a fish; but, right now,
you are in

Jamaica or Cuba with
Assata Shakur.

They giggled
at our kiss & I thought:

now they see the *real*
me, not a poet, just

some pathetic old woman
who made a lover

• 273 •

of a fish. So I reasoned. After all,
you weren't real, you were only

a symbol.

Telly,

I never meant
to betray you. Just

to distract them
as I handed myself

a robe.

When the goddess makes love to me,

she has to pass through my father,
she has to find him
where he sits in a corner inside me
cold as a turd.
I can't reach him anymore.
I don't have the strength to yank him out
& blow on his breasts.
She has to tuck her fingers between his thighs
& warm him, slowly—
first the shoulders & the tops of his arms.
She has to coax the crying boy
to come through the dead
walking on tiptoe.
Sometimes he can't find his way
feeling in the dark with his blunt
fingers,
& sometimes he stands there, dumb-
struck, his body trembling between
us like a little bird's.

Untitled

Ten days after her death, i nap on my mother's
bed &   for the first time it seems in years   in
front of the gentle eyes of the Blessed Virgin (my mother's
Palm Sunday palms folded behind the frame) i feel my
clitoris throb   *aroused?   in my mother's bed?*
before the Virgin?
i press my thighs together as if my hands must
remain clean   i touch the tip of my
left breast until the nipple grows hard & lifts
my thighs tighten   embraced
in this pleasure
as in a prayer that goes up from my whole body
i have gone beyond some dirtiness
some act i cannot conceive my mother would have
condoned   yet   here   now
i have touched some deeper female presence
that her death gives me as a gift

The night I stopped singing like Billie Holiday

Coming to one's voice is . . . not a linear process, not a matter of learning skills, forms, and laws of grammar and syntax. It is a dynamic process in which much of what is occurring and has occurred remains invisible.

THE BLACK NOTEBOOKS

I was playing a CD and enjoying her voice, taking Richard home and talking about the difference between Billie Holiday early and late, and I was thinking about which songs of hers I could learn and sing when I read with the drum player in DC. Just before Richard got out, I said, "You never heard me sing like Billie Holiday, did you?" "No," he said, "but Ben Shannon said that on the first night of class, you closed your eyes and sung a cappella, and that there had never been anything like it."

Alone, driving home with the roof of the car open, feeling that wonderful softness and openness of the summer night, I was deciding whether I should turn down my street and into the gated parking lot or just turn up Billie and keep driving, driving over one or two of the beautiful yellow bridges of Pittsburgh, so architecturally perfect—like the large-scale bridges of New York, the Brooklyn and GW, but small-scale, doable, all of them nearly empty on a summer night, so that you could have the bridge all to yourself. Imagine a bridge all yours on such a night, like a beautiful woman. During the movie, for some reason, I had put my hands under my arms, and I had felt my own body, that beautiful, fat curve under a woman's arm that is also an extended part of the breast, the soft, full crease, and I liked feeling that in myself, as I might like feeling it in another woman, and when I pulled my hand out I could smell myself on it. I was beginning again to have an odor, the juices, the sexual juices, were starting to come back, so that, once again, I would attract or repel like some flower.

Then, right before I turned into my driveway, a terrible premonition came that, if I opened my mouth and started singing, I wouldn't sound like Billie Holiday.

For years that sound had exuded out of me, as if she were in there just waiting for me to open my mouth. Always, there was the strain. Some part of me clamped down on top of what was coming up, and it seemed that is what made Billie happen—I thought even Billie had had that slight squeeze—but something had changed and, when I started to sing, I didn't sound like her.

• • •

I don't remember ever hearing *me* sing—I think it must have been me singing—characterless. I sounded like any person with an OK voice, but nothing special. Before, even if I wasn't as good as Billie, at least I sounded like her, and there was such an aching try—like the pain that made her turn a note into something sweet, short, and unforgettable— that people could feel it. They had been mesmerized. They said maybe I should stop writing poetry and go on the road as a Billie Holiday impersonator. Now my phrasing was off, like somebody trying to win a Billie Holiday contest; the twin-ness had broken, and I sounded like her stranger. My body had forgotten what was most natural for it to do, as if the only way I could be Billie was by not being me.

• • •

There is a story I heard from a South American Indian that, when someone dies, you have to cry for a year; your tears are the boat that carries that person across the waters, and, after a year, when they reach the other side, they are not the person you loved anymore, they are your ancestor.

Every crossing is like that, the great loss of leaving one shore and heading out to nowhere. It is a frightening thing to give up something, even if it is an imitation—especially if you are famous for it. But what if I don't have a real thing, you think to yourself. And, at that moment, all you know is that you have nothing, that you have lost the only thing you had.

• • •

Everyone in my family said I couldn't sing. From the time I was a baby. "She can't carry a tune in a bucket." "Sing solo, so low we can't hear you." Though the teasing hurt and made me unsure of myself, it also made me feel loved, connected, and special. Maybe I sensed that they needed someone to look down on, that the teasing had done them good. Besides, my voice was so small; it didn't weigh anything against their sureties. My voice would squeak out; but, already, I didn't believe anything I said. I fought them good-naturedly, trying to sing to defend myself, but, usually, I ended up giving them the pleasure of covering up their ears and howling, "No, no, no more, please." Being an object of their teasing was a way of hoping something worse wouldn't happen.

• • •

This past week, I went to a concert by Sweet Honey in the Rock. The next day a friend called and said Ysaye Barnwell wants to meet you. She says she's quoting *The Black Notebooks* in a piece she's writing, and she wants to talk to you about it.

I went down to the bookstore where she was signing her book, *No Mirrors in My Nana's House*, and she put her arms around me in a big sister hug. "I'm going to quote that part where you say the development of the voice is not linear. I was writing about this very thing in the voices of singers. We're saying exactly the same thing."

It strikes me as wonderful and terrifying—and obvious—that the voice of the poet is very much connected to the voice of the singer; perhaps, in the most basic way, voice equals voice.

And suddenly I see my voice inside my chest, it's a little child, perhaps the age of a toddler, I don't know if it's a boy or girl, but it's hiding under a rock. Ysaye said that the voice is meant to fill all of space. It's a powerful thing to fill up all of the space outside us with our voices, but, first, we have to be able to fill the space inside. And yet isn't hiding a useful thing? Don't we hide what we are afraid to lose or have taken away? And when it's time, perhaps we see the thing hidden, and then we make a choice about what to do with it.

• • •

I began to listen to Billie Holiday when I was fourteen. I listened for hours every day. I learned every song, nuance, turn, I sang with the records. I sang with her for twenty years; she was always with me. I loved her, though I didn't understand her life, and though I learned things that confused me: that when she spoke, she spoke in a harsh, coarse manner, cursing, with a bitter tongue, her words flat, broad-stroked; that eloquent voice that came when she started singing was from another universe in her throat.

It reminded me of a story about a dentist my husband used to go to. He had palsy, and when his patients saw him coming toward their mouths with the looming buzzsaw in his trembling hand, they were ready to jump out of their seats. However, as soon as he set the instrument on the ridge of one tooth, his hand became perfectly steady. Now I think, for Billie, one voice didn't have anything to do with the other, or perhaps one voice had to be the opposite of the other, or perhaps they were controlled by different brains: the genius brain that put a billion bits of information in the turn of a grace note was not the same brain that said, "Put the god damn glass down mother fucker." From where did that genius brain drink? What did it have access to? Did the one brain know about the other?

• • •

A friend brings me a present before I leave town. I had told her about my voice being like a child, hiding under a rock in my chest, and she hands me, gift-wrapped, a palm-sized, iridescent rock with streaming colors in it—as if it has a hurricane inside—taped to the top of a cassette of lullabies. Music to comfort the child and a rock that holds the power of wind and water: now I am both under it and holding it in my hand.

• • •

Days later, I decide to do a reading for no other reason but joy, no other reason than to have fun. My mother, son, and grandson are in the audience, and I decide to open with my favorite Billie Holiday song. I say, "This is a reading dedicated to love, love exquisite and love hard, and I'm going to begin by singing Billie Holiday's 'Deep Song.'"

Lonely grief is hounding me,
Like a lonely shadow hounding me . . .

I realized something I had forgotten, that meaning is not in the words, but in the sounds; that if we just sing the sounds we put in, the listener will get all the complexity. For that is how we wrote the words, with our hearts singing, and we must not flatten out meaning, must not destroy or deaden, we must let out all the sounds, so that what we said and meant with our whole body can be heard. And in that spirit I sang my reading and, after, I received a standing ovation; never have I received applause like that. No one told me, "You sound like Billie Holiday," but many said, "You have a beautiful voice." My mother said that when I had said I was going to sing, she almost stood up and said, "No, please don't"—she was very afraid she was going to be embarrassed—but when I opened my mouth, she couldn't believe it. She thought I must have had voice lessons.

• • •

It wasn't like Billie's—though it did sound as if I was squeezing up something in me, and that did sound a bit like her—the way she asked men to beat her up before she went on stage so that she would remember the pain—but mine was more open at the throat, so that something came up that was me, and Billie didn't interfere.

When I touched her

When I touched her for the first
time I swooned with
wonder, for the full lips swelled, a dark
fruit bloomed under my
fingers. I could not
breathe with my hand there.
She let me stroke the
lips inside the
lips, that double swelling beneath the
clitoris like the violin's under-
tone, which lifts the whole body from its
anal seat. She
moaned without thought
& spoke to guide me higher, so that my fingers could
find the hill whereon the goddess looked out
with equanimity & calm.

A little prayer to Our Lady

so all day i
go by the
xmas tree bulb (orange) in the
little altar of
shells
that i set up &
keep lit at the
top of the stairs, so that rising now i
rise
to praise
her, to
remember the sacredness of my
work.
perhaps she likes orange light
thrown softly against her for
she looks divine.
my house seems richer
more alive
less lonely
with her here
i am allowed
to believe.

Cherry blossoms

I went down to
mingle my breath
with the breath
of the cherry blossoms.

There were photographers:
Mothers arranging their
children against
gnarled old trees;
a couple, hugging,
asks a passerby
to snap them
like that,
so that their love
will always be caught
between two friendships:
ours & the friendship
of the cherry trees.

Oh Cherry,
why can't my poems
be as beautiful?

A young woman in a fur-trimmed
coat sets a card table
with linens, candles,
a picnic basket & wine.
A father tips
a boy's wheelchair back
so he can gaze
up at

heaven.
         All around us
the blossoms
flurry down
whispering.

    Be patient,
you have an ancient beauty.

                    Be patient,
            you have an ancient beauty.

PART III
The Undertaking

The exigencies of form

It is not the corpse, it is not the artifact, it is the soft thing with feathers. It is hope, it is what is said at the tenderest point; it is covered up with language and syntax, it is metered and measured, it has on its finest dress; it may look like a king going out on a fine horse, or a diplomat in a car with black windows; it may cover itself and hide, but it is reaching, it is alive.

The undertaking

My brother Jay, my half-brother, eighteen years younger than I am,
brings our father's ashes when he visits me in Pittsburgh. They have been
on a shelf in his basement for twenty years, wrapped in the kind of plain
brown wrapper universally understood to be hiding something "dirty."
We slash open the paper to uncover a drawer-shaped plastic box. Jay
pulls a string and the top pops off as easily as the lid on a box of oatmeal
and reveals, too quickly, the chalky issue, the pebbles of our father.

We have walked to the neighborhood golf course—my father loved
golf more than anything good for him—and decide to drop him off at
the top of a little bridge over a spout of clear water. Jay pours most of
the ash, I run down to dislodge the fallen plastic bag from a few prickly
weeds and shake out a half-cup more. We hold each other around the
waist and Jay says his prayer of the moment, "Rest here now safe near
your daughter. Whatever you did, whatever you have done, God chose
you to be our father for a good reason. We love you and will never forget
you." I feel a vacancy, a quiet that may signal an end. I court nothing, no
drama, and yet I wait to see if it's over, really over.

• • •

Many abused children never love again, never trust. Their hands pass
it down to their children. The body holds memories; it will never be
caught again. Talk isn't enough. You can never comprehend. At some
point something happens: a door closes, your boyfriend goes out for a
smoke, and, in less than a second, your stomach tightens like a grill.
Alarm bells ring in the amygdala: Daddy's home.

• • •

Is it possible to change everything that has happened by looking at the
past in a different way? Not denying anything but, perhaps, inserting
some detail that pries open the heart so that more light floods out of it?

• • •

How do you end a book? How do you end a lifelong obsession? Writing itself is a triumph; it changes the past by changing the act of repression. It cries out against violence. It confronts the command to subjugate oneself. When you have been silent, dead for so long, encased and buried, the oppressor's voice is the first one you hear. It is the way you speak to yourself. Then the most childish voice arises. It has to start from the same place it was buried.

• • •

I took my first poetry workshop when I was twenty-seven. The first time I heard "Daddy" by Sylvia Plath, I was shocked and profoundly awakened. I didn't know there was any place, any way for such fury to be expressed, and I had no idea that such an expression could be made into something that had order and beauty, where the broken pieces could make sense. The poem could not only hold an unspeakable truth, it could also bring forth the very voice that had been put down, it could bring it to life.

• • •

You don't just write a book, you live it. I know a book is finished when I've changed. The obsession lifts, it lets me go, a door to the outside world opens. Only the creation of a work of art can spring the trap; only the girl locked inside knows when the door slams open, when the power is enough.

• • •

My mother would look back from the door when she stood up from scrubbing (always the last thing to do was to scrub your way out) and assess the rightness of it. Perhaps she would go back to move an object, adjust a chair an inch, or wipe a spot on the blinds or lampshade; then she would go back and look again—the aesthetics of making something shine. I believe that image stayed in her mind, as a page of a finished poem stays in mine.

• • •

Seventy years ago, the year I was born, Richard Wright wrote of being beaten and abandoned, of his humiliations and tortures in childhood at the hands of his parents, of his lifelong mental suffering, and how these experiences fueled his writing. He describes the voices warring inside him: "In the main we are different from other folk in that, when an impulse moves us, when we are caught in the throes of inspiration, when we are moved to better our lot, we do not ask ourselves: 'Can we do it?' but: 'Will they let us do it?' Before we black folk can move, we must first look into the white man's mind to see what is there, to see what he is thinking, and the white man's mind is a mind that is always changing." I think of the lessons my father taught me. He was born ten years after Wright's birth, his violent and handsome mother brought up in the Colored Children's Industrial Home; his grandmother, born shortly after slavery. How many generations does it take to undo history?

• • •

When I knew I would not "get well," that I would never be the girl my parents wanted, that no matter how much therapy I did and how many books I wrote, I was stuck with myself, that I had to accept my past and live with it; then I knew my parents' struggles. They too battled demons that they couldn't make go away, no matter how much they suffered, no matter what they did or said, no matter how much they wanted to love me and be good.

• • •

Then I gave them credit for what they did right, for what they accomplished: the weekly salary, the food on the table, the beauty of face, for understanding the contours of delicacy, of speech; and for the inner strength: the piercing gray-green eyes that saw good and evil, the gravedigger's determination and necessity.

• • •

Then, too, I realized that my fear, that knee-jerk response, has a twin, an aspect that arises from the same infant sprout: the part that forgets sorrow and is out in the world playing, that notices the first gold light lying on the airy branches of the willow in spring—an image that comes unbidden.

• • •

There is a picture of my father holding me when I was just a few months old. We are standing in front of the bungalow my family shared with my aunt and uncle until I was seven. Above my father's head, you can see the window in the one large finished area of the attic where we lived, a door and thin wall away from bare wood beams and summer's blistering heat. I don't remember why someone snapped us; perhaps it was a celebration—my mother's birthday was in July, I would have been four months old—my father is in a casual shirt with open collar and plain pants, a working man's clothes. There we are in that first public document: I with a look of obvious discomfort, perhaps even the smugness of a little judge; and he looking off-balance, as if someone had just thrown him a bundle of live snakes. He doesn't know what to do with me. What part of himself does he not know how to hold? My lips are sealed, almost puckered in displeasure. I am either not yet afraid to show my feelings, or else the very brain doesn't know enough yet to hide me. He too looks inexperienced; in tenderness and violence, he is a novice, a beginner, a baby.

• • •

Once in a dream I saw my father as a pasty white dog, starved, ignorant, graceless; I said to myself, that is what evil looks like. As I grew stronger, my father grew weaker, until a frightened boy lived inside me. "Rest here now safe near your daughter." In bringing myself forth, I had become his protector.

● ● ●

the poem is change
the poem in change
the end of the poem is change
to change in the poem
to change by the poem
to hold the change
in the poem
to be changed by the poem
(the poem is change)
to change by writing the poem
(the writing is change)
to hold the change in the writing
to hold the change by writing
to breathe through the change
to write through the change
to breathe by writing
to write by breathing
to change by breathing
the change is breathing
to hold the breath
to hold the writing
to hold the change
to hold it

& let it go.

ACKNOWLEDGMENTS

Some of the new poems in this book were previously published in the following magazines. I am grateful to the editors.

American Poetry Review: "The intimates," "Homage," "As my writing changes I think with sorrow of those who couldn't change," "After the Gwendolyn Brooks reading," and "Watching a roach give birth on You-Tube, I think of Lucille Clifton meeting God"; *Birmingham Poetry Review*: "Biographia Literararia Africana," "New Orleans palmetto bug," "My father in old age," "Pantoum for the Broken," "Streaming," "Lauds," "Midnight: Long Train Passing," and "The Peaches of August"; *Lips*: "Black woman as magician at CVS," "The most surprising and necessary ingredient in my mothers spaghetti sauce," and "The Glimpse"; *Missouri Review*: "What are you?"; *The New Yorker*: "I give in to an old desire"; *Poem-a-Day*, Academy of American Poets: "Elegy for my husband" and "The blessed angels" ("Blessed angels"); *Poems for Jerry: A Tribute to Gerald Stern*: "Jerry Stern's friendship"; *Poetry*: "Speculations about 'I'"; *Prairie Schooner*: "To the reader on publication of poems about the abuse in my childhood" ("An apology to the reader"), "Bad Dad," and "On knowing a woman who excuses herself from the table, even in restaurants, to brush her teeth"; *Tin House*: "Gifts from the dead" and "Telly redux: Sharon asks me to send a picture of little fishie Telly"; *Under a Warm Green Linden*: "*La fille aux cheveux de lin.*"

I am especially grateful to ones who nurtured the young poet in me. I daily remember those who have passed on, who provided a safe space: Eleanora Ports, Isabelle Tucker, Amanda LaCroix, Clarence Robinson, Fred Schwartz, and Bruce Derricotte; and all who fed my early joys, especially my cousins Olivia Abner and Sylvia Hollowell.

Much love and gratitude to my families; to supporters who listened, understood, and helped me when I needed help; and to all who made the writing of these poems possible. With special thanks to my editor,

Ed Ochester, for the genius of his vision of American poetry, and for his gentle touch on my psyche at just the right moment throughout the years.

I am most grateful to the universe for the community of Cave Canem. We imagined a place in which black folks were safe to write the poems they needed to write. I send enormous love to the fellows, to all who gave (and give!) of their gifts, and worked (and work!) so hard to make that space happen.

I am grateful to our poetry forbearers, and to all of our ancestors, for the gift of survival.